# Mealtime Mor

## 164 Faith-Filling Entrees to Stir Family Discussions

# Mealtime Moments

164 Faith-Filling Entrees to Stir Family Discussions

## by
## Crystal Bowman
## Tricia Goyer

Tyndale House Publishers, Wheaton, Illinois

Heritage Builders

# MEALTIME MOMENTS

ISBN: 1-56179-801-0

A Focus on the Family book published by Tyndale House Publishers, Wheaton, Illinois.

For Lightwave

Concept Design and Direction: Rick Osborne
Managing Editor: Elaine Osborne
Text Director: K. Christie Bowler
Art Director: Terry Van Roon
Desktop Publisher: Andrew Jaster
Editorial Assistants: Mikal Clarke, Ed Strauss

Cover Design: Steve Diggs & Friends, Nashville

Printed in the United States of America

00 01 02 03 04 05/10 9 8 7 6 5 4 3 2 1

# Contents

# How to Use This Book

Busy, busy, busy! Many families today are on the go so much that it's hard to get everyone around the dinner table long enough to share a meal, let alone hold a meaningful conversation. If this describes your family, make the most of the times when you *are* together. Use these brief readings to grab everyone's interest and get them interacting in lively, often hilarious, conversation!

*Mealtime Moments* deals with both unusual and everyday topics in a creative way, and is designed to provoke interesting, animated discussions. And with all the fun, your kids will be learning important things about the Christian life.

Want to know how to use this book? Here's how! After announcing the title, read the Mealtime Prayer suggestion and have one of your children pray it. Then read the Appetizer. The Appetizer is just that—something to whet your appetite for more. Follow it with the Main Course. This contains the "meat" of the section.

Once you've given your family something to chew on, it's time for Table Talk. These challenging questions will make your kids think about what they've just learned and explain how to apply it to their daily lives. Finally, end with Vitamins and Minerals—a Bible verse that relates to the day's reading and discussion.

How can you get the most out of this book? Be flexible. You don't have to go through it from cover to cover. You might want to use the index to find a topic that

relates to what's happening in your family. For example, forgiveness might be today's big topic, but a mealtime that deals with that topic might be 20 pages past the page you'd planned to read.

And besides these "regular" readings—some of which are pretty irregular and wild!—we've included two extra sections: Holidays and Theme Meals. Kids will especially enjoy these! Be sure to leaf through these sections in advance so you know what's coming up. Plus, a few of them require a minimal amount of preparation.

Be sensitive to how your children respond. Allow enough time for them to answer the questions, but don't force conversation if they don't seem interested. That usually won't be a problem, however. These readings will stir up animated conversations and have your children looking forward to the next meal. Have fun!

# Mealtime Devotions

# In a Pickle?

**Mealtime Prayer:** Give thanks to God that He is with us in all situations and will guide and direct our lives.

**Appetizer:** How many kinds of pickles can you name? What is green and bumpy and red all over? (*Answer: A pickle with a sunburn.*)

**Main Course:** Ever gotten yourself into a pickle? Not a bumpy, green pickle, of course, but a difficult situation. What happened? The Bible gives examples of people who got themselves into "pickles" and how God helped them:
  • Daniel ended up in a lion's den because he prayed, but God kept the lions from hurting him (Daniel 6).
  • Jonah disobeyed God and ended up inside the belly of a big fish (yuck!). He prayed to God and the fish spit him out (Jonah 2).
  • When Paul and Silas were in prison for preaching the gospel, they prayed and sang hymns of praise. God sent an earthquake and their chains fell off (Acts 16).
  • Who deserved their "pickles" and who didn't? Why?

**Table Talk:**
  • How do we sometimes end up in a pickle?
  • What did the Bible characters above do to get out of trouble? What should we do?
  • How can God help us get out of our pickle?

**Vitamins and Minerals:** "Is any one of you in trouble? He should pray. Is anyone happy? Let him sing songs of praise" (James 5:13).

# Let's Go Fishin'

**Mealtime Prayer:** Ask God for opportunities to share your faith and bring others to Him.

**Appetizer:** Name all the ways that it is possible to catch fish.

**Main Course:** Have you ever gone fishing? If so, what bait did you use? How many fish did you catch? Imagine you caught five hundred in an hour. How could it have happened? Read the story of an exciting fishing trip in Luke 5:4–11.

**Table Talk:**
- How did the men catch so many fish?
- How are people like fish?
- What did Jesus mean when He told the disciples they would catch men?
- What kind of bait can we use when we fish for people?
- Where can we go fishing for people?

**Vitamins and Minerals:** "'Come, follow me,' Jesus said, 'and I will make you fishers of men'" (Matthew 4:19).

# Aromatherapy

**Mealtime Prayer:** Ask God to help your life be a sweet smell—be pure and acceptable to Him.

**Appetizer:** Have each person share his or her favorite smell. Which do you prefer: the smell of food or the smell of flowers? Why?

**Main Course:** Why do you enjoy pleasant aromas? What aromas remind you of certain things or events in life?

The Bible tells us that God enjoys pleasant aromas too. When Noah came out of the ark and offered a sacrifice, "the LORD smelled the pleasing aroma" (Genesis 8:21).

Imagine your life is an aroma and everything you do and say is part of your aroma. What would your life aroma be like? Why?

**Table Talk:**
- If kindness had an aroma, what would it smell like? Why?
- How do you think God feels when we send pleasing aromas to Him?
- How can you make your life smell nice?

**Vitamins and Minerals:** "Do not forget to do good and to share with others, for with such sacrifices God is pleased" (Hebrews 13:16).

# Bee Attitudes

**Mealtime Prayer:** Ask God to help you "bee" what He wants you to "bee."

**Appetizer:** Do you know how bees make honey? They eat pollen and mix it with their saliva and put it in their honeycombs! Think of as many words as you can that rhyme with the word *bee*.

**Main Course:** Why do people use the phrase "busy as a bee"? What do bees do that keeps them so busy?

Every bee has a special job, and each bee does what it's supposed to do without grumbling or complaining. Do you think they have good "bee attitudes"? (Imagine a bee complaint box. What might it contain?)

The teachings in Matthew 5:3–12 are called the Beatitudes. Read what these verses have to say about attitudes.

**Table Talk:**
- What does the word *blessed* mean?
- How can we be happy when we are having problems?
- How can changing our attitude help us to be happy instead of sad or angry?
- How can you turn a disaster into an adventure? (*Answer: With a good attitude.*)

**Vitamins and Minerals:** "Blessed is he who trusts in the Lord" (Proverbs 16:20b).

# Free Refills

**Mealtime Prayer:** Think of ways that God provides your family with what you need. Thank Him for providing these things for you.

**Appetizer:** Set a pitcher of water on the table. Have everyone guess how many glasses the pitcher of water will fill. Then fill everyone's glass. Whose guess was the closest?

**Main Course:** Read the story of a poor widow in 2 Kings 4:1–7.

Why did the oil stop when all the jars were full? What do you think would have happened if she had collected more jars? If the widow had come to you for jars, how many would you have given her?

**Table Talk:**
- How does God provide for poor people today? How can you be part of that?
- How does God provide for you?
- How is the widow's oil like God's blessings?

**Vitamins and Minerals:** "Now to him who is able to do immeasurably more than all we ask or imagine, according to his power that is at work within us, to him be glory in the church and in Christ Jesus throughout all generations, for ever and ever! Amen" (Ephesians 3:20–21).

# Bull's-Eye

**Mealtime Prayer:** Thank God that He is always with us and that we never have to be afraid.

**Appetizer:** The giant Goliath was over nine feet tall. How many people from your family would have to stand on each other's shoulders to be as tall as Goliath?

Goliath's armor weighed about 125 pounds. How many kids in your family would he have to have carried around to equal that weight?

**Main Course:** Imagine facing a giant. What would you want to help you? David, a young shepherd boy, was brave enough to fight a giant. Read the exciting story of David and Goliath in 1 Samuel 17:32–50.

**Table Talk:**
- What did David take to help him fight Goliath?
- How did David get his courage?
- What would you have done if you were David?
- What kinds of giants do we face in our everyday lives?
- What weapons can we use to give us courage?

**Vitamins and Minerals:** "Be strong and courageous. Do not be afraid or terrified because of them, for the LORD your God goes with you; he will never leave you nor forsake you" (Deuteronomy 31:6).

# Water, Water Everywhere

**Mealtime Prayer:** After the leader prays each phrase, everyone says, "We thank You, dear Lord."

> Leader: For food to eat and water to drink,
> For healthy bodies and minds that think,
> For all that we have and all we enjoy,
> For every girl and every boy.

**Appetizer:** Try to come up with 10 uses for water. Go!

**Main Course:** Eat as much of your dinner as you can without taking a drink. How long could you last? Why do we need to drink? What makes us thirsty? When do you most appreciate an ice-cold glass of water?

**Table Talk:**
- Jesus is called the "Living Water." How is He like water? Why do we need Him?
- Where can we find "living water"? How can we drink "living water"?
- Why does the satisfaction of "living water" last forever?

**Vitamins and Minerals:** "Whoever drinks of the water I give him will never thirst. Indeed, the water I give him will become in him a spring of water welling up to eternal life" (John 4:14).

# Time-out

**Mealtime Prayer:** Thank God for times to rest and worship. Thank Him for your church, the minister, and the leaders of your church.

**Appetizer:** What would happen if people worked every day and never took a day off? Why do we need a day of rest?

**Main Course:** What different types of churches have you been to? What is your favorite place of worship? Why do we need to take time to worship God?

**Table Talk:**
- In the Ten Commandments, God tells us to remember the Sabbath day to keep it holy. What does that mean?
- What did God do on the seventh day after He created the world? If God doesn't get tired, why did He take a day off?
- Think of 10 good reasons to go to church.

**Vitamins and Minerals:** "Let them exalt him in the assembly of the people and praise him in the council of the elders" (Psalm 107:32).

# You've Got Mail!

**Mealtime Prayer:** Name some missionaries you know. Ask God to bless and protect them as well as other missionaries throughout the world.

**Appetizer:** When was the last time you wrote a letter? When was the last time you received a letter?

   If someone collected your letters and put them in a book, what kind of book would it be: mystery, romance, adventure?

**Main Course:** What is the most famous collection of letters ever written? (Hint: They're in the Bible.) The apostle Paul traveled to many places, from Rome to Syria, telling people about Jesus. He didn't stay in one place very long, so he wrote letters (now in the New Testament) to keep in touch with the new Christians. Why do you think he wanted to keep in touch with them?

**Table Talk:**
   • Would anyone besides the friend you're writing to be interested in your letters?
   • How are Paul's letters different from yours?
   • If you got a letter in the mail from a very wise person, how would you treat it?
   • Paul's letters are messages from God to you. How should you treat them?

**Vitamins and Minerals:** "I thank my God every time I remember you" (Philippians 1:3).

# Not Like Ice Cream

**Mealtime Prayer:** As you thank God for your food today, thank Him that He is eternal and that His love is everlasting.

**Appetizer:** Who is the oldest person you know? Do you know what animal lives the longest? (*Answer: The turtle. Some live for more than one hundred years.*)

**Main Course:** At the beginning of your meal, place a small scoop of ice cream in a bowl. What happens to the ice cream while you eat your dinner?

Ice cream doesn't last long, does it? Name some other things that don't last very long. Name some things that *do* last for a long time.

The Bible says that God is everlasting. What does that mean? What are some things about God that are everlasting?

**Table Talk:**
- What difference does it make in our lives that God is everlasting?
- How do we know that God will always be alive?
- How are Christians everlasting?

**Vitamins and Minerals:** "Before the mountains were born or you brought forth the earth and the world, from everlasting to everlasting you are God" (Psalm 90:2).

# Mud Pie

**Mealtime Prayer:** "Thank You, Lord, for the food we eat, for our family and the friends we meet. Each is special and unique! Amen."

**Appetizer:** Can you name three types of dirt? (*Answer: Sand, silt, and clay.*) The main difference between them is their size. If a particle of sand were the size of a basketball, silt would be the size of a baseball, and clay would be the size of a golf ball![1] What would your yard look like if dirt was really that size?

**Main Course:** Is there a special place where you can dig in the mud? What do you like to make out of mud?

When did God play in the mud? When He formed Adam out of dirt! Read Genesis 2:7–8.

**Table Talk:**
- Why do you think God "formed" Adam instead of simply speaking him into existence like the other creatures?
- If you formed all the food on your plate into the shape of a man, could you make him come alive? Why or why not?
- How did God's "breath of life" make man different from the animals?
- What do you think God enjoyed most about forming you?

**Vitamins and Minerals:** "The LORD God formed the man . . . and breathed into his nostrils the breath of life, and the man became a living being" (Genesis 2:7).

[1] Soil types: http://www.urbanext.uiuc.edu/gpe/case2/c2facts2.html

# Plain Ol' Vanilla

**Mealtime Prayer:** Let each person offer his or her own kind of prayer—short or long, silent or aloud. Have the last person thank God for your different tastes in prayer—and food!

**Appetizer:** Which ice cream flavor is the top seller: Strawberry, Cookies 'N' Cream, Chocolate, or Vanilla? (*Answer: Vanilla.*) What's your favorite flavor?

**Main Course:** Why isn't there just one flavor of ice cream? If you were ice cream, which flavor would you be: Mysterious Mocha, Cheery Cherry, Quiet Kiwi, Grumpy Grape, or Outrageous Orange? Why?

Why didn't God make just one kind of person? All of us have different "tastes." Your flavor is what makes you *you.*

Each of us has a different way of praying and worshiping God, too. Some like to sing praises. Some are champs at quoting Bible verses. Others would rather sit quietly and think about God's goodness. All these are part of your flavor.

**Table Talk:** Take a vote on the following questions:
- Would you rather sing a praise song with motions or without?
- Would you rather pray standing up, sitting, kneeling, or bowing with your face to the floor? Why?
- Now that you've voted, should you all have to sing and pray in the ways that got the most votes? Why or why not?

**Vitamins and Minerals:** "There are different kinds of service, but the same Lord" (1 Corinthians 12:5).

# Soul Food

**Mealtime Prayer:** (Tune: "Amazing Grace")
"Amazing grace, how great Thou art, You meet my every need.
You quench my thirst, You guard my home, my soul and body feed."

**Appetizer:** Did you know it can take as long as 12 hours for a meal to get through your digestive system? That's because your small intestines are four or five times taller than you are![2] Look around and find something that tall. Would it fit inside you?

**Main Course:** How is the phrase "you are what you eat" true? What happens to your body when you eat nutritious food?

Besides food, what other things do you feed on throughout the day (television, music, friends, etc.)? Which of these please God? Do these things strengthen you or weaken you? How?

One good thing we can feed on is the Bible. God's Word can be thought of as food for your soul. Why does absorbing God's truths into your life give you strength?

**Table Talk:**
- Name five things you can "absorb" from the Bible. How do they become a part of you?
- What sort of music feeds the soul?
- What sort of music, movies, or games hurt your soul? Why?

**Vitamins and Minerals:** "You are strong, and the word of God lives in you" (1 John 2:14).

---

[2] Ask Jeeves Web site: http://www.askjeeves.com (Ask question about digestion.)

**BIBLE/CHOICES/GOOD EXAMPLE**

# "Bible" for a Hundred, Alex

**Mealtime Prayer:** Do you find yourself praying the same words every meal? The way God designed things (including the Bible) shows that He enjoys variety. Add new words to your mealtime prayer. For example: How would you describe your favorite hobby? Interesting? Fun? Action-packed? Can you apply any of these to God?

**Appetizer:** Did you know that the Bible was written over a period of about 1,500 years? If you lived for 1,500 years, what hobbies would you take up?

**Main Course:** Turn your meal into a *Jeopardy* challenge round. Appoint one person to be Alex Trebek. Use these statements as game starters, then think of some of your own. (Your answer needs to be a question!)

Q: There are 39 of them in the Old Testament and 27 in the New Testament.
*A: What are the books of the Bible?*
Q: The Gospels were named after these four men.
*A: Who are Matthew, Mark, Luke, and John?*
Q: This is a book of songs and praises.
*A: What is the book of Psalms?*

**Table Talk:**
- What are five things you can tell others about your favorite hobby?
- What are five things you can tell others about the Bible?
- Why is it important to know Bible facts?

**Vitamins and Minerals:** "The word of God is living and active" (Hebrews 4:12).

# Mystery Revealed: Almonds and Donkeys!

**Mealtime Prayer:** You can use Bible verses as prayers. Pray this one: "O LORD, you are my God; I will exalt you and praise your name, for in perfect faithfulness you have done marvelous things" (Isaiah 25:1).

**Appetizer:** Did you know that almonds are related to peaches? With a peach, the flesh is eaten and the pit is thrown away. With an almond, the pit is eaten and the flesh (hull) is thrown away!

What would happen if you got them backward? How would they taste?

**Main Course:** True or false? Answer these questions.
- God made a stick blossom and produce almonds (Numbers 17:8).
- God used bones to bring a dead man to life (2 Kings 13:21).
- God used a sling and rock to defeat an army (1 Samuel 17:50).
- God used a donkey to deliver a warning (Numbers 22:28–30).

Answer: They're all true! God made Aaron's stick bud, Elisha's bones heal, and David's sling hit a bull's-eye. God also caused Balaam's donkey to speak! What other things has God used to do His work?

**Table Talk:**
- What does it mean for your life that God can do anything? How does it make you feel?
- Try to think of something God hasn't done yet. Then imagine ways He could do it.

**Vitamins and Minerals:** "With man this is impossible, but with God all things are possible" (Matthew 19:26).

# Have It Your Way

**Mealtime Prayer:** "Bless me, O Lord, and let my food strengthen me to serve You for Jesus Christ's sake. Amen." —Isaac Watts[3]

**Appetizer:** Did you know that ketchup and cheese are the most favored hamburger toppings? What do you like on your hamburger? Why?

**Main Course:** Have you heard the fast-food restaurant slogan "Have it your way"? What does it mean to you? Why do customers like having choices? Did you know that in the Bible there are stories of men who told God, "Have it Your way"?

**Table Talk:**

- How did Noah let God "have it His way" when it came to building the ark? Could a canoe have done the job? Why? (See Genesis 6:14–22.)
- How did Moses let God "have it His way" when he went before Pharaoh? What was the result? (See Exodus 7:1–6.)
- How did Joshua let God "have it His way" when he marched around Jericho? Did it make sense at the time? Why? What did God prove? (See Joshua 6:1–21.)
- What are some ways you can let God "have it His way" in your life today?

**Vitamins and Minerals:** "It is God who arms me with strength and makes my way perfect" (Psalm 18:32).

---

[3] *Bless This Day*, compiled by Elerida Vipont (Harcourt, Brace, & World), 1958, 19.

# Freshly Squeezed

**Mealtime Prayer:** Do a "squeeze prayer." Holding hands, have each person thank God for His love, then gently squeeze the next person's hand when finished.

**Appetizer:** Did you know that freshly squeezed orange juice can last up to 40 days in your refrigerator if stored in an airtight container? Think of five other fruits that can be squeezed for their juice. Which is your favorite?

**Main Course:** Parents brought their little children to Jesus, and He took them into His arms and blessed them. You can read about it in Mark 10:13–16. How do you think Jesus' special attention made those children feel?

**Table Talk:**
- Close your eyes and imagine Jesus squeezing you. What would it feel like? What would you tell Him? What do you think He would say to you?
- Why do you think Jesus said we must receive the kingdom of heaven like a child? How do children receive gifts?
- Why was Jesus angry with His disciples? What might they have learned when they saw Jesus with the children? What have you learned about the way Jesus loves each of us?

**Vitamins and Minerals:** "Jesus said, 'Let the little children come to me, and do not hinder them, for the kingdom of heaven belongs to such as these'" (Matthew 19:14).

# The Whole Enchilada

**Mealtime Prayer:** Unless you're ill, there is only one way for your meal to travel to your stomach (through your mouth), and there is only one way for you to travel to God (through Jesus). Thank God for these special paths.

**Appetizer:** Bible quiz time!
1. The payment (wages) for sin is (Romans 6:23): a. Death; b. Sickness; c. A fine
2. Jesus came to earth (John 3:16, 1 Corinthians 15:3): a. To show you how much He loves you; b. To take the punishment for your sins; c. Both of the above.
3. God will forgive me (1 John 1:9): a. When I learn to always do the right thing; b. When I admit I've done wrong, and believe that Jesus died for me; c. When I become an adult.
4. You can get to heaven (John 14:6): a. On a jet plane, breaking the sound barrier; b. By being a good person and doing good deeds; c. By putting your faith in Jesus Christ and asking Him into your heart. (*Answers: a, c, b, c*)

**Main Course:** Jesus is the whole enchilada. That is, He's all it takes to become God's child. Compare Jesus to three other types of food. (Example: Like spinach, Jesus gives us strength.)

**Table Talk:**
- What other things do people put their faith (trust) in instead of Jesus?
- Will any of these help them become a part of God's family?
- What can you tell someone who wants to know the way to heaven?

**Vitamins and Minerals:** "Jesus answered, 'I am the way and the truth and the life. No one comes to the Father except through me'" (John 14:6).

# Souper-De-Dooper!

**Mealtime Prayer:** Say the alphabet-soup prayer: "A–B–C–D–E–F–G. Thank You, God, for feeding me." Thank God for other ways He cares for you.

**Appetizer:** Did you know that, on average, Americans buy 290,520 cans of Campbell's® soup per hour? The first archaeological evidence of someone stirring up soup dates back to 6,000 B.C. The main ingredient was hippopotamus bones![4] What would you say if you were served that for dinner? Think up other soup ingredients.

**Main Course:** Has a family member ever made you a bowl of soup when you were sick? Why? How does soup make you feel better?

God likes to take care of you, too. Luke 12:6–7 says, "Are not five sparrows sold for two pennies? Yet not one of them is forgotten by God. Indeed, the very hairs of your head are all numbered. Don't be afraid; you are worth more than many sparrows." Why would God care about your hair?

**Table Talk:**
- God feeds, clothes, and protects you. Does knowing this warm you up inside? In what other ways does God meet your needs?
- The Bible says that God knows the number of hairs on your head. What other weird things does God know about you?

**Vitamins and Minerals:** "The Lord is good, a refuge in times of trouble. He cares for those who trust in him" (Nahum 1:7).

[4] Campbell's Soup Web site: http://www.campbellsoup.com

# Ba-Manna Splits (While Supplies Last)

**Mealtime Prayer:** "Come, Lord Jesus, be our guest, May this food by You be blessed, May our souls by You be fed, Ever on the Living Bread."[5]

**Appetizer:** Did you know that manna could be baked, boiled, ground, beaten, cooked in pans, and made into cakes? Do you think the Israelites ever made ba-manna splits? What about ba-manna cream pie? What other things could they have made?

**Main Course:** Throughout the Old Testament, God uses word pictures to represent Jesus Christ. Read Exodus 16. What did God provide for the Israelites who were wandering in the desert? How did it help them?

In the New Testament, Jesus referred to Himself as "true manna." Why? Jesus gives us life and satisfies our spiritual hunger. But His care lasts longer than 40 years. How long?

**Table Talk:**
- Manna fed the Israelites for 40 years. Why did manna show God's people His care?
- What other symbols in the Old Testament did God use to represent Jesus? What do they tell us about God?
- What is your favorite food? How many days could you eat it for breakfast, lunch, and dinner?

**Vitamins and Minerals:** "It is my Father who gives you the true bread from heaven. For the bread of God is he who comes down from heaven and gives life to the world" (John 6:32–33).

[5] Cate: CateHH@aol.com

**THE BIBLE TELLS ONE BIG STORY**

# King-Sized Oven

**Mealtime Prayer:** Thank God for the many ways He takes care of us. Ask Him to give you the courage to obey Him.

**Appetizer:** You've probably said, "I'd give anything for a drink!" or "I'd die for an ice cream." What would you be willing to die for? Chocolate mousse? To score the winning goal? Your beliefs?

**Main Course:** Three young men were willing to die just to stand up. Or were they? Read the thrilling story of three brave men from Daniel 3.

**Table Talk:**
- What was the most exciting part of the story?
- What were they really willing to die for?
- Do you think the three men knew they would not burn up? Why or why not?
- What should we do when someone wants us to disobey God?

**Vitamins and Minerals:** "Obey me, and I will be your God and you will be my people. Walk in all the ways I command you, that it may go well with you" (Jeremiah 7:23).

# Attitude of Gratitude

**Mealtime Prayer:** What are some things that your family members have done for each other today? Thank God for your family and the ways you can help each other.

**Appetizer:** How do you feel when you do something nice for someone else and he or she doesn't thank you for what you've done? What about when someone does something nice for you and you don't thank the person?

**Main Course:** The Bible tells us that one day Jesus healed 10 men who were sick with a disease called leprosy (Luke 17:12–19). Only one of the men took time to thank Jesus for healing him. How do you think Jesus felt about this? Why do you think the other nine men didn't thank Jesus?

Why is it important to say thank you to our friends and family for things they do for us? Why is it important to thank God for what He does?

**Table Talk:**
- What things do we take for granted but should be thankful for?
- How does it help our relationships with one another when we remember to show gratitude?
- Write a thank-you note to someone and give it to him or her tomorrow.

**Vitamins and Minerals:** "Give thanks to the LORD, call on his name; make known among the nations what he has done" (Psalm 105:1).

# Two's Company

**Mealtime Prayer:** Thank God for your friends and family with whom you can share your many blessings. Thank Him also that He is our Father and that we can have a personal relationship with Him.

**Appetizer:** God created us so that we would enjoy being with others. Take turns naming things that you enjoy doing with others and saying why.

Can you enjoy being with someone even though you're not doing anything special? Why or why not?

**Main Course:** Have you ever felt lonely? Why do you think we have lonely feelings? What is a sure cure for loneliness?

When there is no one else around, are we really alone? Why or why not? Who is with you? How do you know?

**Table Talk:**
- What is the best thing about having God always with you?
- If God is our friend, how can we be friends to Him?
- What can we do for someone we know who is lonely?
- What can we do if we are lonely?

**Vitamins and Minerals:** "We proclaim to you what we have seen and heard, so that you also may have fellowship with us. And our fellowship is with the Father and with his Son, Jesus Christ" (1 John 1:3).

# Words and Bees

**Mealtime Prayer:** "[Dear Lord Jesus,] may the words of my mouth and the meditation of my heart be pleasing in your sight" (Psalm 19:14).

**Appetizer:** Have each person taste a drop or two of honey. How does it taste? When someone calls you "Honey," does it mean that:

    a. You are thick and syrupy?
    b. You were made by bees?
    c. You are sweet and pleasant?
    d. You belong on a biscuit?

**Main Course:** There is a saying that goes, "Sticks and stones may break my bones, but names will never hurt me." Is it true? Why or why not?

How can words hurt us? How can our words hurt others?

The Bible says that pleasant words are sweet as honey and healing to the bones. How can words be sweet as honey? How can they be healing?

**Table Talk:**

- Why does God want us to use sweet words?
- What should we do if our words have hurt someone?
- Say something kind to someone at your table.
- What kind words can you say to someone tomorrow? (Be sure to do it!)

**Vitamins and Minerals:** "Pleasant words are a honeycomb, sweet to the soul and healing to the bones" (Proverbs 16:24).

# True or False?

**Mealtime Prayer:** Thank God for the Bible and the messages He gives us in His Word.

**Appetizer:** Each person think of a message, true or false, that you want to give. It could be "Mom is beautiful" or "lions eat grass" or anything. Decide whether each message is true or false.

**Main Course:** How did you decide which messages were true or false? When someone tells us something, how can we know whether he or she is telling us the truth?

There are many messages in the Bible. Some were written by prophets who talked about things that were going to take place in the future. How did the prophets know what to write? How can we know whether they were true?

For example, the prophet Isaiah predicted that the Messiah would be born. Was this true? Why or why not? How do we know that everything in the Bible is true?

**Table Talk:**
- What should we do with the messages in the Bible?
- What message in the Bible has not yet come true?

**Vitamins and Minerals:** "The prophet who prophesies peace will be recognized as one truly sent by the LORD only if his prediction comes true" (Jeremiah 28:9).

# Hide-and-seek

**Mealtime Prayer:** Thank God that He is always with us, that He watches over us, and that He always knows where we are.

**Appetizer:** What game do mice like to play? (*Answer: Hide-and-squeak.*)

**Main Course:** Let's play a quick game of hide-and-seek. Have one person hide. Everyone else must try to find the person who is hiding. Come back to the table when the person is found.

How long did it take to find the one who was hiding? Why couldn't we see the person who was hiding until we searched for a while? What special abilities would we need in order to see someone at all times? How can God see us no matter where we are? How can God see everyone at the same time?

**Table Talk:**
- If you could be in two places at the same time, where would you be?
- What difference does knowing that God can always see us make in how we live? Give some examples.

**Vitamins and Minerals:** "Nothing in all creation is hidden from God's sight" (Hebrews 4:13).

# Kids Rule!

**Mealtime Prayer:** Pray for the leaders of our country, that they would be good examples and do right in the sight of God.

**Appetizer:** Who is the youngest teacher that you know? The youngest pastor? Who was the youngest man to become president of the United States? (*Answer: Theodore Roosevelt at age 42.*)

If you became president, what changes would you make? Why?

**Main Course:** Choose a child to be the leader for five minutes. He or she will tell the others what to eat and when to eat. (You may want to let children take turns.)

How does being the leader feel? How does it feel when you are not the leader? Which would you rather be? Why?

A boy named Josiah became the king and leader of Judah when he was only eight years old. The Bible tells us that Josiah did right in the sight of the Lord (2 Kings 22:2). What do you think that means?

**Table Talk:**
- How can you be a good leader at home? With your friends?
- How could you help the country serve God? (Hint: See the Vitamins and Minerals.)

**Vitamins and Minerals:** "If my people, who are called by my name, will humble themselves and pray and seek my face and turn from their wicked ways, then will I hear from heaven and will forgive their sin and will heal their land" (2 Chronicles 7:14).

# Cold Feet

**Mealtime Prayer:** Think of times when God has helped you to have courage. Thank God for the courage He gives us.

**Appetizer:** Have someone get a bucket of ice-cold water while everyone else takes off their socks and shoes. Now have each person take turns putting his or her feet in the bucket of water. How does it feel to have cold feet? What is another meaning for "cold feet"?

**Main Course:** The Bible tells the story of a man named Peter who got cold feet one night—both kinds! He saw Jesus walking on top of the water and decided to join him. As he walked out on the water toward Jesus, the cold waves were tossing around him and the wind was blowing fiercely.

Imagine being in his place. How would you have felt? What would you have done?

Peter became frightened and began to sink, but Jesus reached out His hand and caught him (Matthew 14:25–31).

**Table Talk:**
- When do you get "cold feet"?
- How can Jesus help us when we are afraid?
- How can we help others who get cold feet?

**Vitamins and Minerals:** "My help comes from the LORD, the Maker of heaven and earth" (Psalm 121:2).

# The Brain Game

**Mealtime Prayer:** Thank God that He is holy and righteous. Ask Him to help your minds dwell on things that are pleasing to Him.

**Appetizer:** Here is an exercise for your brain: Decide together what is lovely or admirable about each person at your table.

**Main Course:** Have each person share a favorite activity and tell why he or she enjoys it.
What kinds of activities help us think about things that are positive? What kinds of activities might influence our thoughts in a negative way? Why is it important for us to stay away from things that might give us sinful thoughts?

**Table Talk:**
- God is holy and righteous. What does that mean?
- Why should we try to be holy and righteous?
- How can we dwell on things that are good rather than things that are bad?

**Vitamins and Minerals:** "Brothers, whatever is true, whatever is noble, whatever is right, whatever is pure, whatever is lovely, whatever is admirable—if anything is excellent or praiseworthy—think about such things" (Philippians 4:8).

# Dirty Dishes

**Mealtime Prayer:** Choose someone to read the following prayer:
"Thank You, Father, for the food You give us every day.
Thank You for forgiving us and washing our sins away. Amen."

**Appetizer:** Count how many dishes are on your table, including the utensils. How clean are they?

**Main Course:** After you finish your meal, describe what the dishes and utensils look like. Can you tell what you had to eat by what's sticking to the plate? Which food made the most mess? By looking at the empty glasses, can you tell what you had to drink? Why do you wash the dishes, glasses, and utensils before using them again?

**Table Talk:**
- How do our lives become dirty and messy like the dinner dishes?
- Could someone tell where you've been or what you've done by looking at your life or listening to you?
- How do you think God feels about using "dirty dishes"?
- If you're a "dirty dish," how can you get clean?
- How can you stay clean?

**Vitamins and Minerals:** "Create in me a pure heart, O God, and renew a steadfast spirit within me" (Psalm 51:10).

# Hungry? Try These Chicken Nuggets!

**Mealtime Prayer:** "For food in a world where many walk in hunger/For faith in a world where many walk in fear/For friends in a world where many walk alone/We give You humble thanks, O Lord. Amen."

**Appetizer:** Why don't chickens play sports? (*Answer: Because they hit fowl balls.*)

**Main Course:** Have you ever had someone call you a chicken? Can you think of a person who's never been afraid? God knew that each of us would face times of fear. That's why He gave us "nuggets of truth." Guess how many times the Bible says, "Do not be afraid." Is it 10, 50, or 70 times? (*Answer: 70.*)

What things does the world tell you to worry about? Read Isaiah 43:5; Luke 2:10; and Revelation 1:1–18. What do these verses tell us? With promises like that, you can give worries to God and leave chicken for the barbecue!

**Table Talk:**
- How does knowing God is with you help? Why?
- Was there a time this past week when you were afraid? What did you do?
- Name one worry you can give to God right now.

**Vitamins and Minerals:** "My peace I give you. I do not give to you as the world gives. Do not let your hearts be troubled and do not be afraid" (John 14:27).

# SOS

**Mealtime Prayer:** When you pray, ask God to help you be willing to learn from others in everything you do.

**Appetizer:** Did you know that "dice" means to cut in cubes, and "whip" is to "beat into a froth"? What are some other cooking words you know?

**Main Course:** Have you ever needed help reading a recipe? Words like *dice* and *whip* can be confusing. Sometimes the Bible can be confusing too!

Read Acts 8:30–31. Why didn't the Ethiopian understand God's Word? After Philip explained the passage, what did the man do? Why is it important that we help each other understand God's Word?

### Table Talk:
- What could have happened if the Ethiopian had said, "I can handle it"?
- What might have happened if Philip had said, "I can't help"?
- Who helps you understand God's Word?
- Who can you help understand God's Word? How?

**Vitamins and Minerals:** "You yourselves are full of goodness, complete in knowledge and competent to instruct one another" (Romans 15:14).

# Man Missing For 10 Years...Found!

**Mealtime Prayer:** Pray this verse, "The LORD is my shepherd, I shall not be in want" (Psalm 23:1).

**Appetizer:** Sheep are curious but dumb animals. Did you know that sheep are often unable to find their way home even if the sheepfold is within sight? Knowing this, the shepherd never takes his eyes off his wandering sheep. Read Psalm 32:8.

**Main Course:** Set the table with one less plate than needed. Hide the plate, and then ask your family to look for it. Celebrate when you find it.

Read the story Jesus told about finding something that was lost. It is in Luke 15:4–7. What does "repent" mean? Why should we celebrate when a person repents?

**Table Talk:**
- Why does God look for lost people?
- Why was the plate important? Why was the sheep important? Why is each person important?
- Why do you think Jesus used stories to tell us about His kingdom? How do these stories help us to understand?
- What do you think a party in heaven is like?

**Vitamins and Minerals:** "We had to celebrate and be glad, because this brother of yours was dead and is alive again; he was lost and is found" (Luke 15:32).

# I'll Take Mine Sunny-side Up

**Mealtime Prayer:** Philippians 1:4 says, "In all my prayers for all of you, I always pray with joy." Pray over your meal with joy.

**Appetizer:** Give each child two paper plates. On one plate, have them draw a happy face. On the other, have them draw a sad face.

Read the following statements. The children should raise their happy-face plates if it's a way to share joy and raise their sad-face plates if it is not a way to share joy.

1. Appreciate a gift.
2. Pout when you don't get your way.
3. Introduce yourself to a new boy or girl at school.
4. Complain about dinner.
5. Share a toy with a smile.

**Main Course:** Have you ever eaten an egg "sunny-side up"? That's when the bright yellow yoke is facing up. It looks like the sun's shining on the world.

What could it mean when your face is "sunny-side up"? When was your face "sunny-side up" today? Why?

**Table Talk:**
- Where does all joy come from?
- What things has God done that should make you smile?
- Think of other ways your attitude can be "sunny-side up" today. Call them out.

**Vitamins and Minerals:** "Your love has given me great joy and encouragement, because you, brother, have refreshed the hearts of the saints" (Philemon 1:7).

# Bring Out the China—Company's Coming!

**Mealtime Prayer:**

"Lord Jesus, be our holy guest,
Our morning joy, our evening rest,
And with our daily bread impart
Your love and peace to every heart. Amen."[6]

**Appetizer:** Did you know that in the White House, the State Dining Room can seat 140 people? In 1902 Theodore Roosevelt decorated that room with hunting trophies. He hung a moose head over the fireplace![7] If your parents let you, how would you decorate your dining room?

**Main Course:** What would you do if you knew the president of the United States was coming to your house for dinner? What would you fix?

We have someone even more important than the president visiting us every day. Who? If you have an extra chair at your table, set a place for the King of Kings.

**Table Talk:**

- How can you daily prepare your heart for God's visit?
- How can you make God a special part your daily life, including your mealtime?
- If Jesus were at your table, what would you serve Him for dessert?

**Vitamins and Minerals:** "Here I am! I stand at the door and knock. If anyone hears my voice and opens the door, I will come in and eat with him, and he with me" (Revelation 3:20).

---

[6] Christopher Health: sparky@camtech.net.au
[7] The White House for Kids Web site: http://www.whitehouse.gov/WH/kids/html/home.html

# Featuring: The Greatest Commandment, Part 2

**Mealtime Prayer:** "I'll try my best to live this day, By the Golden Rule in every way! Amen."

**Appetizer:** Did you know that "Love your neighbor as yourself" is sometimes called "the Golden Rule"? Why is it "golden"? Bible authors showed love by listening to God and by sharing His Word.

**Main Course:** What would happen if you bought a new kitchen appliance and there were no directions included? Would you be able to use it safely? Why are directions important? What did God give us His directions in? What "appliance" are they for?

For your kitchen appliance, the two most important directions may be: (1) remember to plug it in, and (2) do not stick your fingers in any moving parts—Ouch! What are the two most important directions of the Bible? Read Matthew 22:37–39.

**Table Talk:**
- What one word will help you remember the two most important directions?
- What does loving God this way look like?
- How can you love your family as yourself right now?

**Vitamins and Minerals:** "Jesus replied: 'Love the Lord your God with all your heart and with all your soul and with all your mind.' This is the first and greatest commandment. And the second is like it: 'Love your neighbor as yourself'" (Matthew 22:37–39).

# Garbageman to the Rescue!

**Mealtime Prayer:** Have someone read the following prayer:
"God, our Father, we thank You in prayer,
For forgiveness, for family, for food that we share. Amen."

**Appetizer:** Did you know that if you emptied a typical garbage can, you would find 38 percent paper, 14 percent metal, 8 percent plastic, 4 percent food waste, and 2 percent glass?[8] What are the most common things your family throws away?

**Main Course:** Did you know that God makes a good garbage man? What types of things does He like to remove from your heart and mind (jealousy, anger, etc.)? What does God do when you ask Him to help remove the garbage? How do you feel afterward? Thankfully, God's sin-disposal service comes more than once a week. In fact, it's available anytime you ask!

**Table Talk:**
- What are some words you can use to describe garbage?
- What type of garbage tends to collect in your heart?
- What would you like God to remove right now? Ask Him to do so.

**Vitamins and Minerals:** "If we confess our sins, he is faithful and just and will forgive us our sins and purify us from all unrighteousness" (1 John 1:9).

[8] Garbology Web site: http://www.extension.umn.edu/

**FORGIVENESS/SIN**

# Menu: Jumbo Shrimp

**Mealtime Prayer:** "Lord, thank You that a shrimp like me is jumbo in Your eyes! Amen."

**Appetizer:** Did you know that people in the United States are eating twice as much shrimp as they were ten years ago? Among seafood, shrimp's popularity is second only to tuna.[9] What is your favorite seafood? Why?

**Main Course:** Read Luke 19:5–10. Zacchaeus was a "shrimp." He was of "small stature." What did he have to do to see Jesus? What does this tell you about Zacchaeus's heart? How did Jesus reward him?

**Table Talk:**
- Do you have a friend who is seeking God? How do you know he or she is seeking God? What can you say about Jesus to show your friend that Jesus is what he or she is looking for?
- Your friend may not be climbing trees, but he or she might be asking questions about Jesus, church, or the Bible. What example does Jesus give about dealing with people who are seeking? Remember that every seeker of truth is "jumbo" (a big fish) in God's eyes!

**Vitamins and Minerals:** "Anyone who comes to [God] must believe that he exists and that he rewards those who earnestly seek him" (Hebrews 11:6).

[9] http://www.earthsummitwatch.org/shrimp/index.html

# Would You Like Fries with That New Life?

**Mealtime Prayer:** Ask God to work in you today so others see that He has given you a new life.

**Appetizer:** When you're completely healthy, how do you feel? Happy? Like you can take on the world? What's the worst thing about being sick?

Jesus often showed people His love and power by healing them. What is your favorite Bible story about healing? After dinner, act out this story with your family. How will you show excitement when you are healed?

**Main Course:** In one Bible story, after healing a young girl, Jesus tells her parents to give her something to eat. Read Luke 8:49–55.

**Table Talk:**
- Imagine you were that girl. What would it have been like to be that sick? To be healed by Jesus?
- Why would Jesus ask the parents to feed the girl? What food do you think the parents fixed? What would you have asked your parents to fix?
- Jesus doesn't only heal bodies. What else does He heal?
- Has Jesus ever healed you? When?

**Vitamins and Minerals:** "The Son gives life to whom he is pleased to give it" (John 5:21).

# Chicken or Egg?

**Mealtime Prayer:** "Lord, we are truly grateful for the food before us. Thank you for the . . . [take turns thanking God for the foods on your table]. Amen."

**Appetizer:** How do you think the first Lifesaver® candy was invented? The machine Clarence A. Crane was using to produce a new kind of mint candy malfunctioned and punched a hole in the center. It was an accidental invention.[10] What firsts did you have this last year?

**Main Course:** Are you a first-rate Bible scholar? Answer these firsts.
- What was Christ's first miracle? (*Answer: Turning water into wine, John 2:3–11.*)
- What was the first food God gave Adam in the garden? (*Answer: Every seed-bearing plant, Genesis 1:29.*)
- When was the first time God told someone to store food? (*Answer: When Noah was packing the ark, Genesis 6:21.*)
- What came first, the chicken or the egg? (*Answer: The chicken, Genesis 1:20–21.*)

**Table Talk:**
- Why would God record all these firsts?
- The Bible passages mentioned above are about God's care for people. What do they tell us about God?
- How else does God provide?

**Vitamins and Minerals:** "He makes grass grow for the cattle, and plants for man to cultivate—bringing forth food from the earth" (Psalm 104:14).

---

[10] *The Book of Lists for Kids*, Sandra & Harry Choron (Massachusetts: Houghton Mifflin, 1995), 175.

# Need an Eraser?

**Mealtime Prayer:** Thank God for your meal and all that He provides for you. Praise God that He is perfect and that He never makes mistakes.

**Appetizer:** Have someone get a pencil for everyone to look at. Which end of the pencil is used for writing? What is the other end used for? Why do we need both ends of the pencil?

**Main Course:** What things besides pencil writing do you wish you could erase? Why? Does God ever use an "eraser"? Why or why not? What are some perfect things that God has done? How would things be different if God made mistakes or changed His mind from time to time like people do?

**Table Talk:**
- How does knowing God is perfect help you?
- If God is perfect, why isn't the world?
- If God knows we are not perfect, what do you think He expects from us?
- When will we be perfect?

**Vitamins and Minerals:** "I will proclaim the name of the LORD. Oh, praise the greatness of our God! He is the Rock, his works are perfect, and all his ways are just" (Deuteronomy 32:3–4).

# Be a Bookworm

**Mealtime Prayer:** Have someone read the following prayer:
"Your Word, O Lord, teaches me truth.
Your Word shows me the way.
Help me to learn; help me to listen.
Help me, O Lord, to obey. Amen."

**Appetizer:** Name some of the books each of you has read in the past week. What kind of books do you enjoy reading the most? Why? If someone said he would put you in prison for reading a certain book, what would you do?

**Main Course:** The Bible is an all–time best-seller! Why do you think so many people read it? What are some things we can learn from reading it? How is the Bible different from other books?

**Table Talk:**
- How important is the Bible to you? Why? Would you read it even if you'd go to prison? (This is a real possibility in some countries.)
- How can reading the Bible help us make decisions in our everyday lives?
- If we believe what the Bible says, how does that affect how we treat others?
- Why do you think it is important to memorize Bible verses?

**Vitamins and Minerals:** "I have hidden your word in my heart that I might not sin against you" (Psalm 119:11).

# Baa, Baa, Black Sheep

**Mealtime Prayer:** Thank God for being your Shepherd and for wanting you in His flock.

**Appetizer:** True or false? There are more sheep in Australia than people. (*Answer: True.*) What would your house be like if there were more pets than people in it?

**Main Course:** The Bible often refers to God as our Shepherd. Name things that a shepherd does. How is God like a shepherd? How is being a shepherd like being a pet owner? How are you like sheep?

**Table Talk:**
- If God's the "pet owner" and you're the "pet," how does He treat you? Why?
- How do you feel, knowing God's looking out for you?
- How are you different from a pet? How does God treat you differently than a pet owner? Why?

**Vitamins and Minerals:** "He tends his flock like a shepherd: He gathers the lambs in his arms and carries them close to his heart" (Isaiah 40:11).

# Spread the Mustard

**Mealtime Prayer:** As you thank God for your blessings, ask Him to give you faith to believe in His Word and to trust Him in all things.

**Appetizer:** If you have a jar of mustard seed in your spice cabinet, place a few seeds on a plate and set them on the table. How big is a mustard seed? Compare it to other items. Did you know that the oil from mustard seeds is used for making soap? What are some other possible uses for mustard seeds? Be creative.

**Main Course:** The Bible says that if we have faith the size of a mustard seed (that's not very much!), nothing will be impossible for us (Matthew 17:20). If by believing you could make something true, what would you believe? Why?

**Table Talk:**
- Where does faith come from?
- What things are true whether you believe them or not? How do you know?
- What can you believe in that is absolutely true and reliable?
- How can faith give you peace and confidence?

**Vitamins and Minerals:** "Now faith is being sure of what we hope for and certain of what we do not see" (Hebrews 11:1).

# Scrambled or Fried?

**Mealtime Prayer:** Thank God that He has a plan and purpose for your life. Ask Him to use you according to His will.

**Appetizer:** Place a carton of eggs on the table. Talk about the different ways that eggs can be used. How do you like your eggs prepared? If you were an egg, how would you like to be used?

**Main Course:** Eggs look very similar, but they can be used for many different purposes. How are Christians like eggs? How does God use Christians in different ways? If God can do anything, why does He use Christians? What would happen if all Christians were used in the same way?

**Table Talk:**
- How do you think God decides who He is going to use and how He will use them?
- What do we need to do in order for God to use us?
- What special job do you think God has planned for you?

**Vitamins and Minerals:** "There are different kinds of gifts, but the same Spirit. There are different kinds of service, but the same Lord" (1 Corinthians 12:4–5).

**SERVICE**

# Flying Backward

**Mealtime Prayer:** Thank God for His Word, and that He is able to do the impossible.

**Appetizer:** Did you know that hummingbirds can fly backward? It's hard to understand how that is possible, isn't it? Think of some other things that are hard to understand.

**Main Course:** Here are some facts about the Bible that will boggle your mind. True or false?
- It was written in five languages. (*False. Three languages.*)
- It was written over a period of 1,500 years. (*True.*)
- It was written in many different countries on three continents. (*True.*)
- The authors came from all walks of life and most of them knew each other. (*False. Few knew each other.*)

If each member of your family wrote a set of rules for how you should get along, how similar would they be? In the Bible, 40 people from different families came up with very similar rules. How do you think they did that?

**Table Talk:**
- The 40-plus writers of the Bible agreed on many things. Why?
- How did they know what to write?
- How did they know about things that would happen in the future?
- If you could write a book for the Bible, what would you write about?

**Vitamins and Minerals:** "In the past God spoke to our forefathers through the prophets at many times and in various ways" (Hebrews 1:1).

# Caterpillar or Butterfly?

**Mealtime Prayer:** Thank God for His salvation and that He changes lives.

**Appetizer:** The caterpillar spins its cocoon with silk. What other creature spins with silk? (*Answer: The spider spins its web with silk.*)

**Main Course:** A caterpillar is not always a caterpillar. It eats and eats until it is full. Then it spins a silky cocoon around itself and goes to sleep. When it wakes up and comes out of its cocoon, it is a new creature—a butterfly.

If you could go to sleep and wake up different, what would you be? Why?

How is Saul in the New Testament like a caterpillar? Read Acts 9:1–22 to find out.

**Table Talk:**
- Are you a caterpillar or a butterfly? Why?
- How do people change when they become Christians?
- When you meet someone, how can you tell if he or she is a Christian?
- How can people tell that you are a Christian?

**Vitamins and Minerals:** "If anyone is in Christ, he is a new creation; the old has gone, the new has come!" (2 Corinthians 5:17).

# Nicknames

**Mealtime Prayer:** Have someone read the following prayer:
"Dear Father, You are Lord and King, Almighty Creator of everything.
Messiah, Counselor, Prince of Peace, May your blessings never cease. Amen."

**Appetizer:** Reverse the first and last letters of your name. What do you get? (Examples: Mark=Karm, Chris=Shric.)

**Main Course:** Do you have a nickname? If so, what is it? Do your parents ever call you Honey, Buddy, or Sweetie Pie? What other names do they call you? Why do we have nicknames?

Some people have names that refer to their job, such as doctor or officer. Think of other names or titles that describe what people do.

God has many different names too. Some of God's names describe His character or what He's like, such as holy and almighty. What are some other names that describe God?

Some of God's names describe what He does, such as Creator or Savior. What are some other names that describe what God does?

**Table Talk:**
- Why do you think God has so many names?
- Using the letters of the alphabet, think of more names for God (for example, A=Almighty).
- If you had to choose a name to describe yourself, what would it be?

**Vitamins and Minerals:** "And He will be called Wonderful Counselor, Mighty God, Everlasting Father, Prince of Peace" (Isaiah 9:6).

# Quiet, Please!

**Mealtime Prayer:** Ask God to help you live at peace with one another and to be kind and thoughtful to each other. Thank Him for your family and for the blessings He has given you.

**Appetizer:** Have one person take a sheet of paper and draw a line down the center of the paper. On one side of the paper, write down some harsh words people use. On the other, write some gentle words they give you. What kinds of feelings go with saying and hearing the harsh words? What about the gentle words?

**Main Course:** Proverbs 15:1 says, "A gentle answer turns away wrath, but a harsh word stirs up anger." Why do people use harsh words? How do you feel when someone uses them with you? What is a gentle answer? How can a gentle answer help settle an argument? How do you feel when someone uses gentle words with you?

**Table Talk:**
- What should we do if we get into an argument?
- How can we disagree without arguing?
- How can you be a peacemaker?
- Why would God want us to be peacemakers?

**Vitamins and Minerals:** "Blessed are the peacemakers, for they will be called sons of God" (Matthew 5:9).

# Better Than Homemade

**Mealtime Prayer:** Thank God for the many ways He provides for you. Thank Him for being the Bread of Life.

**Appetizer:** Name all the different kinds of bread that you can think of. What is your favorite?

**Main Course:** Have everyone at the table eat a piece of bread. How does it taste? What do you like with it (butter, cheese, liver, ketchup, etc.)?

Breads of various forms are eaten all over the world by almost everyone. Why do so many people eat bread? What are some of the different ways people use bread? (For example, in Ethiopia they use it as a plate!) How is it good for us?

The Bible says that Jesus is the Bread of Life. What do you think that means? How is the "Bread of Life" different from regular bread?

**Table Talk:**
- Where can we find the bread that Jesus has to offer?
- How do we fill ourselves with the Bread of Life? How is this bread good for us?
- How can we offer the Bread of Life to others?

**Vitamins and Minerals:** "I tell you the truth, he who believes has everlasting life. I am the bread of life" (John 6:47–48).

# The Big Apple

**Mealtime Prayer:** Along with thanking God for your food, also thank Him for the people who shared a "seed of faith" with the members of your family (people who told you about Jesus). Who were these people?

**Appetizer:** Did you know that apples are a member of the rose family? What did Johnny Appleseed share at the same time he was sharing his apple seeds? (*Answer: Jesus.*)

**Main Course:** Did you know that the apples from one tree can fill 20 boxes every year?[11] How many seeds do you think are in those 20 boxes? Someone said, "You can count the seeds in one apple, but you can't count the apples in one seed." Think about it. What does this mean?

When you tell your friends about Jesus, you share seeds of faith with them (1 Corinthians 9:11). What can happen with these seeds? How are your friends like "the apples in one seed"?

**Table Talk:**
- When you tell someone about Jesus, how many lives could you be affecting? Will you ever know? When?
- What's one very cool thing you can share about Jesus?
- What do you like best about apples?

**Vitamins and Minerals:** "Other seed fell on good soil, where it produced a crop—a hundred, sixty or thirty times what was sown" (Matthew 13:8).

[11] Dole Web site: http://www.dole5aday.com/encyclopedia/apple/apple_facts.html

# Is It Possible? Starving Man Refuses Bread

**Mealtime Prayer:** Pray Psalm 75:1, "We give thanks to you, O God, we give thanks."

**Appetizer:** If you had the power to do so, what food would you make appear before you right now? Why that food?

**Main Course:** Have you ever been really, really hungry? When? What was it like? Once, Jesus went 40 days and 40 nights without food! Imagine how hungry He must have been. How would you handle that kind of hunger?

The devil thought this would be the perfect time to trick Jesus. Read Matthew 4:3–4. How did Jesus answer Satan? Why do you think it worked? How do you think Satan feels about the Bible? Why?

**Table Talk:**
- Think of a time you were tempted. How did you handle it? How well did it work?
- How could you handle temptation like Jesus did?
- How can knowing the Bible help you?

**Vitamins and Minerals:** "Everything that was written in the past was written to teach us, so that through endurance and the encouragement of the Scriptures we might have hope" (Romans 15:4).

# Warning: No Snacks Before Dinner!

**Mealtime Prayer:** "Lord, help me to remember that Your timing is perfect. Amen."

**Appetizer:** Did you know the word cookie actually comes from the Dutch word *koekje*, pronounced "kook-ya," which means "little cake"?[12] Why do you think they gave it this name?

**Main Course:** Have you ever sneaked a treat before dinner? Your stomach is growling. Your patience is wearing out. You munch a cookie (or two or three) just to ease your hunger. What happens when dinnertime arrives? What if you were served your favorite meal, and you were too full to enjoy it? How would you feel? What are the benefits (and hard parts) about waiting?

**Table Talk:**
- How is eating snacks before dinner like filling your life up with what you think is best?
- What are some things you want to "fill up on" that God might say "don't eat" or "wait" to?
- Why is God's timing and "food" best? Why can you trust Him?
- How can you remind yourself to wait for God's best?
- Write out the word *koekje* on a piece of paper. Underneath it, write out 5 things you will trust God and wait for.

**Vitamins and Minerals:** "As God's chosen people, holy and dearly loved, clothe yourselves with compassion, kindness, humility, gentleness and patience" (Colossians 3:12).

[12] Girl Scouts Web site: http://www.girlscoutcookiesabc.com/pages/abfs_cookietrivia.html

# What's on Your Label?

**Mealtime Prayer:** "Dear Lord, a name isn't something I can see or taste or touch. But help me to remember that it sticks with me wherever I go. Amen."

**Appetizer:** Grab three cans of food from the cupboard. What things on the label make customers want to buy them? If your mom and dad were cans in a supermarket, what good things would you put on their labels? "Hard worker"? "Good cook"? "Generous neighbor"? What labels would you have?

**Main Course:** If you had to choose between "Slimy Green-Grass Pudding" and "Chocolate Delight," which would you choose? How did the name of the label affect your decision?

How are people also labeled by their actions? What labels do we give others? What label do your neighbors know you by?

First Samuel 18:30 says, "David met with more success than the rest of Saul's officers, and his name became well known." David's name is carried on to this day. What good things is David remembered for?

**Table Talk:**
- How will others treat you if your name is respected? If it isn't respected?
- What can you do to make sure you have a good name? (Read Proverbs 3:3–4.)
- What label would you give yourself?

**Vitamins and Minerals:** "A good name is more desirable than great riches" (Proverbs 22:1).

# Super-Size Me

**Mealtime Prayer:** One purpose of prayer is to tell God how wonderful He is. Pray this:
"God is great, God is good, We will thank Him for this food.
By His hand must all be fed, Thanks be to God for daily bread. Amen."

**Appetizer:** Ever had a picnic at the beach? What did the sand get into? The teeth of many Egyptian skeletons are worn down from eating sandy bread. Any guesses why? Too many picnics? In the days when pharaohs ruled Egypt, bread was made from grain called emmer wheat. As the wheat was ground, small bits of sand often got mixed in.

**Main Course:** Read Genesis 41:34–41, 48–49, 53–57. How did God help Joseph? How did Joseph help Pharaoh? How was Joseph rewarded? Who should get the praise, God or Joseph? Why?

**Table Talk:**
- How many things did God provide in this story? What where they? (Hint: not just food.)
- What has God provided for you?
- How are you rewarded when you listen to God? How are the people around you rewarded?

**Vitamins and Minerals:** "[God] provides food for those who fear him" (Psalm 111:5).

# All Ears!

**Mealtime Prayer:** Many families hold hands during mealtime prayer and close their eyes to concentrate on God. Do this today and listen carefully to the one praying.

**Appetizer:** Q: What has ears but can't hear? (*A: A cornfield.*)

What makes popcorn pop? It has more water inside the kernels than regular corn. When it is heated, the pressure of the steam builds and the kernel finally explodes.[13]

When is your favorite time to eat popcorn? How are you similar to popcorn?

**Main Course:** Here's a game to play before dessert that will help you become more like corn—all ears! **1.** Blindfold a child and choose one parent for the child to find. **2.** Place the blindfolded person in the center of the room. Everyone else move to the corners. **3.** Everyone call out directions to their corner. The blindfolded person must follow only the voice of the chosen parent. **4.** Finding the correct corner means the child wins!

**Table Talk:**
- Every day we hear many "voices." What advice do you get from the "voices" of movies? Music? Friends? Whose voice should you follow?
- What type of advice do your parents give? What happens when you concentrate on their words and obey them?
- What is one command that's difficult to obey? Why?

**Vitamins and Minerals:** "Listen, my son, to your father's instruction and do not forsake your mother's teaching" (Proverbs 1:8).

[13] Eat Ethnic home page: http://www.eatethnic.com/FunFacts.htm

# Come on, Slowpoke, Ketchup!

**Mealtime Prayer:** If you hid under the table or behind a chair, could God see you? Of course. Thank God for sticking to you like ketchup sticks to a bun!

**Appetizer:** Did you know that ketchup, or *ke-tsiap*, originally came from China? Ke-tsiap was a tangy sauce made from pickled fish and spices. In the late seventeenth century, English sailors took it back to England. Unfortunately the unusual ingredients were hard to find. Instead of giving up on the idea, cooks tried out flavorings such as walnuts, anchovies, and tomatoes. Imagine that—tomato ketchup![14] What is your favorite thing to do with ketchup?

How fast does Heinz ketchup leave the bottle? Twenty-five miles per year! Talk about slow!

**Main Course:** Have you ever been called a slowpoke? Sometimes we hurry and hurry but never catch up. On the other hand, have you ever had to wait for someone else who was lagging behind? Who is never too slow or too impatient?

Why don't we have to worry about playing ketchup . . . er, catch up . . . when it comes to God?

**Table Talk:**
- Why is keeping pace with others hard?
- What is your pace? What animal would you compare yourself to?
- How does God match your pace? Why?

**Vitamins and Minerals:** "O LORD, do not forsake me; be not far from me, O my God" (Psalm 38:21).

---

[14] Amuze Me Suz: http://www.geocities.com/SoHo/Café/5536/ketchup.html

# Go Ahead, It's Good for You!

**Mealtime Prayer:** Thank the Lord that He has given you food to make your body strong, and His Word to make your spirit strong.

**Appetizer:** Did you know that broccoli has been served up for dinner for at least two thousand years? (Parts of the Bible have been around even longer!)[15]

**Main Course:** Have you ever heard your mom say, "Eat your broccoli; it's good for you"? Believe it or not, your parents put broccoli (or other veggies) on your plate because they love you. What good things are in broccoli? How is the Bible like broccoli? What good things are in the Bible?

Of course, the best part is that the Bible doesn't taste mushy or leave little green things between your teeth! What does the Bible leave you with instead?

**Table Talk:**
- How does eating nutritious foods like broccoli make you feel?
- How does reading the Bible make you feel? Just reading it is not enough. What else do you need to do?
- If you could outlaw one vegetable, what would it be?

**Vitamins and Minerals:** "He took the Book of the Covenant and read it to the people. They responded, 'We will do everything the LORD has said; we will obey'" (Exodus 24:7).

---

[15] Mann's Broccoli Facts: http://www.208.1.230.25/institute/morebroccolifacts.htm

# God-Sized Water Bottle

**Mealtime Prayer:** Pray this verse: "As the deer pants for streams of water, so my soul pants for you, O God" (Psalm 42:1).

**Appetizer:** Did you know that in many places, about 6,800 gallons of water are required to grow a day's food for a family of four.[16] What three other things is water used for?

**Main Course:** Have you ever shared a water bottle on a hot day? Did you get to take as much as you wanted? Why or why not?

It's not like that with God. God is available anytime to give you "a spring of water welling up to eternal life" (John 4:14). If you could find a water bottle big enough for that, what would it be like?

What phrases are true of both Jesus and water?

**Table Talk:**
- Can you pray so often that God doesn't have time for anyone else? Does God ever have to limit His time with you? Why or why not?
- If for one day your parents had no limits on what you could do, how would you want to spend the day?
- God has no limits. How can you spend your days with God?
- How does it help to know that God is everywhere at once?

**Vitamins and Minerals:** "If I go up to the heavens, you are there; if I make my bed in the depths, you are there" (Psalm 139:8).

[16] Brita home page: http://www.brita.com

# Seen by One, Seen by All... They've Been with Jesus!

**Mealtime Prayer:** "Lord God almighty, bless us here today. May we grow in strength and wisdom as we spend time with You. Amen."

**Appetizer:** If you could buy any three toys, what would they be? Why? Where did you hear about these toys? How does watching commercials affect you? How do things we see and hear change how we feel? How do people we hang out with change us?

**Main Course:** Read Acts 4:3–13. After Jesus returned to heaven, what happened to Peter and John? How did they change after being with Jesus? What do you think it was that changed them? Why? They didn't even stop telling people about Jesus when they were put in jail. How did the priest know they had been with Jesus?

**Table Talk:**
- How can your parents tell who or what you've been spending a lot of time with?
- How will others know you've been with Jesus?
- Name three reasons why Jesus is more exciting than toys.

**Vitamins and Minerals:** "When they saw the courage of Peter and John and realized that they were unschooled, ordinary men, they were astonished and they took note that these men had been with Jesus" (Acts 4:13).

**GOOD EXAMPLE/GOOD NEWS**

# 150 Watts

**Mealtime Prayer:** Along with thanking God for your food, thank Him for being the Light of the World. Ask God to let His light shine through you.

**Appetizer:** Have someone volunteer to be blindfolded and then walk around the table. Be careful the volunteer doesn't get hurt! Have him or her take the blindfold off and walk around again. What differences are there between the two?

**Main Course:** If you were in a strange room in the dark, how would you walk around in it? What dangers might there be hidden in the dark?

Some people are afraid of the dark. What could their reasons be?

The Bible says the world is full of darkness because of sin. How is sin like darkness? How can it be dangerous? How does sin keep us from going the right way?

**Table Talk:**
- The Bible also says that Jesus is the Light of the World. What does that mean?
- How can being a Christian help us to see more clearly?
- How can following Jesus keep us from danger?
- How can following Jesus make you a "light"?

**Vitamins and Minerals:** "I am the light of the world. Whoever follows me will never walk in darkness, but will have the light of life" (John 8:12).

# Name That Tune

**Mealtime Prayer:** Use Psalm 150:1–2 as your prayer: "Praise the LORD. Praise God in his sanctuary; praise him in his mighty heavens. Praise him for his acts of power; praise him for his surpassing greatness." Amen.

**Appetizer:** Play "Name That Tune." Have someone hum a song while the others try to guess the name of the song. Keep playing until everyone has had a turn to hum a song.

**Main Course:** What do you enjoy about music? Why? Why do you think there are so many different styles of music? What kind do you like the best? Why would God create us with the ability to sing and play musical instruments?

The book of Psalms is a collection of songs, poems, and praises. Many of the psalms were written to be sung to the music of stringed instruments. How can songs be used for praise and worship?

**Table Talk:**
- Music is powerful. Why does God care about the kind of music we listen to? How does it affect you?
- Make up a praise to the tune of your favorite song, to "Jingle Bells," and to "Row, Row, Row Your Boat."

**Vitamins and Minerals:** "I will sing to the LORD all my life; I will sing praise to my God as long as I live" (Psalm 104:33).

# Blowin' in the Wind

**Mealtime Prayer:** Thank God for the many ways He shows Himself to us and for the wonders of His creation.

**Appetizer:** Have everyone go outside or look out a window. Is the wind blowing? How do you know? Can you see it? Why or why not?

**Main Course:** What would you say to someone who said there was no such thing as wind? How would you prove there was? (What does the wind do? What does it sound like?) How is God like the wind? How can we hear God? What does God do that lets us know He exists?

**Table Talk:**
- Romans 1:20 says, "For since the creation of the world God's invisible qualities—his eternal power and divine nature—have been clearly seen, being understood from what has been made, so that men are without excuse." How can we see God in nature?
- What other things show you God is real?
- What would you say to someone who says you can't prove there is a God?

**Vitamins and Minerals:** "The heavens declare the glory of God; the skies proclaim the work of his hands" (Psalm 19:1).

# "Peas" Pass the Veggies

**Mealtime Prayer:** Thank God that His Word teaches us right from wrong. Ask Him to help you choose what is right.

**Appetizer:** The word *vegetable* contains the word *table*. What vegetables are on your table? If you had to eat only vegetables, what would you choose for breakfast? If you could be any kind of vegetable, what kind would you be? Why?

**Main Course:** Daniel was a young man who loved the Lord. He was invited to a royal feast, but there was a problem. Daniel didn't want to eat the meat because he knew it had been offered to an idol. He decided to eat vegetables instead.

Read what happened in Daniel 1:8–16. How did God honor Daniel for making the right choice?

**Table Talk:**
- Think of times when you had to choose not to do something wrong. What happened?
- How can we know what is right when we face a tough choice?
- How can your conscience and/or the Bible help you know the difference?

**Vitamins and Minerals:** "Love must be sincere. Hate what is evil; cling to what is good" (Romans 12:9).

# Walk a Mile in His Shoes

**Mealtime Prayer:**
> "Help us, dear Jesus, every day
> To follow You in every way;
> To glorify and honor You
> In everything we say and do. Amen."

**Appetizer:** How long would it take for you to walk from one end of your town to the other? What would you want to take with you?

**Main Course:** When Jesus lived on earth, He walked from town to town teaching people about God and healing people who were sick. One day Jesus asked 12 of His friends to help Him. The 12 men who agreed to follow Jesus were called His disciples.

What do you think it would have been like to be with Jesus all day? What would be hard about being a disciple? What do you think the disciples brought with them? What did they have to leave behind?

**Table Talk:**
- If Jesus lived here today, where would you follow Him and how could you help Him?
- What would you leave behind? What would you gain?
- Jesus is here right now. How can you follow Him in your regular life? What will you "leave behind"?

**Vitamins and Minerals:** "Jesus said to his disciples, 'If anyone would come after me, he must deny himself and take up his cross and follow me'" (Matthew 16:24).

**FOLLOWING JESUS**

# Goin' Down!

**Mealtime Prayer:** As you thank God for His blessings, thank Him for the gift of faith and the opportunity to bring others to Him.

**Appetizer:** If you had to cut a hole in your roof, what tools would you need? How long do you think it would take? Why would it be dangerous? What possible reason could make you do it?

**Main Course:** The Bible tells the story of some men who had a great reason to bring down the roof. They wanted to bring their sick friend to Jesus. They knew that Jesus could make their friend better, but they couldn't get near Him because it was too crowded. Read what happened in Mark 2:2–5, 11–12.

**Table Talk:**
- How long do you think it took to cut through the roof?
- Besides wanting their friend healed, why do you think the men did this?
- How is Jesus' response different from what your parents' would be if you cut a hole in the roof? Why?
- How hard would you work to bring your friends to Jesus? How can you do that?

**Vitamins and Minerals:** "It is by grace that you have been saved, through faith—and this not from yourselves, it is the gift of God" (Ephesians 2:8).

# Frogs for Dinner

**Mealtime Prayer:** Use the Vitamins and Minerals verse as your prayer.

**Appetizer:** Write the Egyptian plagues (water turned to blood, boils, frogs, hail, lice, death of cattle, locust, flies, darkness, and death of firstborn) on pieces of paper and put them into a bowl. Take turns choosing a paper then drawing a picture of the plague until someone guesses it.

**Main Course:** How would you try to convince someone to do what you wanted? God had a unique way: The people of Israel were slaves in Egypt. Moses asked Pharaoh to let them leave, but Pharaoh said no. Why would he do that?

God sent plagues to convince Pharaoh to let the people go. After the firstborn in every Egyptian family died, Pharaoh told Moses to get out of town!

**Table Talk:**
- What might have happened if Pharaoh had let the people leave after the first plague?
- Why do you think Pharaoh was so stubborn? What can happen when people think they are greater than God?
- What was God showing Pharaoh, Egypt, and His people about Himself?
- How would you like God to convince you to do things His way?

**Vitamins and Minerals:** "Yours, O LORD, is the greatness and the power and the glory and the majesty and the splendor, for everything in heaven and earth is yours. Yours, O LORD, is the kingdom; you are exalted as head over all" (1 Chronicles 29:11).

# Just Say "Cheese"

**Mealtime Prayer:** Think of some things that make you happy. Thank God for those things.

**Appetizer:** If Swiss cheese comes from Switzerland, where does cottage cheese come from? (*Answer: The grocery store.*) How many different kinds of cheese can you name? What is your favorite? What are cheeses good for?

**Main Course:** Have everyone say "cheese" and smile a big cheesy smile. How do you feel when you smile? Why is smiling good for us? Why are our smiles good for others? Think of 10 reasons why you can be happy. How does being happy affect our relationships with others?

**Table Talk:**
- Do you think God wants us to be happy? Why or why not?
- Often just thinking of what God has done for us makes us happy. What has God done for you that makes you feel happy?
- How can we help others to be happy?

**Vitamins and Minerals:** "A cheerful heart is good medicine, but a crushed spirit dries up the bones" (Proverbs 17:22).

# Good News!

**Mealtime Prayer:** As you thank God for your food, thank Him for the good news, which gives us "spiritual food" for our souls. (Each person name some good news you're thankful for.)

**Appetizer:** Time for a "good news" session. Have everyone take a turn to share some good news from today or this past week. Next, have someone get a newspaper. Read some of the headlines. Does the newspaper tell good news, bad news, or both?

**Main Course:** What are the first four books in the New Testament called? (The Gospels: Matthew, Mark, Luke, and John.) Gospel means "good news." What is that good news? (The story of Jesus and how He came to the world to bring salvation to all people.) Why is this good news? What other good news does the Bible tell?

**Table Talk:**
- Why would we rather hear good news than bad?
- How does the good news of salvation change how I act?
- Name three things we can do with the good news from the Gospels.

**Vitamins and Minerals:** "These things are written that you may believe that Jesus is the Christ, the Son of God, and that by believing you may have life in his name" (John 20:31).

# Puppies and Rainbows

**Mealtime Prayer:** Praise God for His righteousness (moral goodness). Ask Him to help you live lives that are pleasing to Him.

**Appetizer:** Do you like puppies and rainbows? Why or why not? Name some other things that you like. Why do you like them? What are some things you don't like? Why don't you like them?

**Main Course:** The Bible tells us that God has likes and dislikes too. What does righteousness mean? (Right living.) Why do you think God loves righteousness? What are some other things that God loves? What happens when you do those things consistently? Why does God hate sin? What are some of the sins that God hates? What happens when you do those things?

**Table Talk:**
- Sin leads to unhappiness in the long run, if not right away. So, why do people sin?
- Why do you think God wants us to be righteous? (For example, He knows it will make us happy.)
- How do you think God feels when we obey Him? When we disobey?
- How can we be righteous or live right for God? (For example, speak kindly.)

**Vitamins and Minerals:** "Just as he who called you is holy, so be holy in all you do" (1 Peter 1:15).

# Fish Dinner: Sticks to Your Ribs for Three Days!

**Mealtime Prayer:** Sing your prayer today to the tune of "Row, Row, Row Your Boat." "Bless, bless, bless this food, Bless all present here. Help us now to spread Your love To people far and near."

**Appetizer:** The largest whale ever captured was a blue whale measuring 109 feet and 3.5 inches. That's like 29 kids lying in a straight line! That whale was captured near the South Shetland Islands in 1926. What's the biggest fish you've ever seen?

**Main Course:** Read Jonah 1:17–2:10. Why did God send Jonah to Nineveh? How did God get Jonah back on track? Do you think Jonah will ever forget that fish's dinner?

Looking at what happened when Jonah preached (Jonah 3), why was it so important for him to go to Nineveh?

**Table Talk:**
- If you rode in a fish's belly, would you get seasick? What would it be like?
- How might you be like Jonah? What important job could God have for you to do?
- Why should you obey God? What reminds you or helps you do that?
- What could happen if you didn't obey?

**Vitamins and Minerals:** "Remind the people to be subject to rulers and authorities, to be obedient, to be ready to do whatever is good" (Titus 3:1).

**GOOD NEWS/OBEDIENCE/WITNESSING**

# Eggs—actly Like Jesus!

**Mealtime Prayer:** Jesus thanked His Father for His food. We can follow His example by singing this song: (Tune: "London Bridge") "God is great and God is good, God is good, God is good. Let us thank Him for this food. Alleluia!"

**Appetizer:** How long does it take a hen to produce an egg? (*Answer: twenty-four to twenty-six hours.*) What kind of hens produce white-shelled eggs? Brown-shelled eggs? (*Answer: White-shelled eggs are produced by hens with white feathers and white ear lobes, and brown-shelled eggs are produced by hens with red feathers and red ear lobes. Really.*)

**Main Course:** Play an eggs-citing game of charades:
1. Write the names of family members on separate pieces of paper.
2. Put names into a bowl (or plastic eggs, if you have them).
3. Add a half dozen slips with "Jesus" on them.
4. Each family member takes a turn drawing a name to role-play.
5. The person who guesses the answer gets "next ups."
6. Pay special attention to how people portray Jesus.
7. Give everyone a high five for doing an egg-cellent job!

**Table Talk:**
- How do we behave when we're acting like Jesus?
- Is it possible to mimic His actions throughout the day? How?
- Why should you copy Jesus?

**Vitamins and Minerals:** "Whoever serves me must follow me" (John 12:26).

# Got Milk?

**Mealtime Prayer:** Pray the Bible from Psalm 145:15–16. (Have Bible handy so people know what to read.)

Reading: "The eyes of all look to you."
Response: "You give them their food at the proper time."
Reading: "You open your hand."
Response: "And satisfy the desires of every living thing."

**Appetizer:** Did you know that cows are good for more than milk and steaks? What else comes from cows? (Camera film is made from cow bones, and toothpaste and soap come from cow fat!)

**Main Course:** Follow the milk on your table backward to see where it comes from. Your parents may buy milk at the store, but how does it get there? Where do delivery drivers get it? How does the dairy get it out of the cows? What do cows need to produce milk? Who made the grass that cows eat? Who made the sunshine and rain that makes the grass grow? God is responsible for the milk in your glass. The same is true for every other food. God is the ultimate provider!

**Table Talk:**
- What else ultimately comes from God?
- Follow some other things backward. Where did your T-shirt come from? What about your stereo or TV?
- How do things like friendship, happiness, and safety lead back to God?

**Vitamins and Minerals:** "[God] has shown kindness by giving you rain from heaven and crops in their seasons; he provides you with plenty of food" (Acts 14:17).

**GOD'S PROVISION**

# No Mis-steaks!

**Mealtime Prayer:** Thank the Lord that in His perfection He made wonderful things, like the Bible, good food, and your family!

**Appetizer:**
- Q: People in what area of the United States consume more steaks in restaurants than people in any other region in America? (*Answer: The Southeast.*)
- Q: How many people wrote the Bible? (*Answer: More than 30.*)
- Q: What was the first book to be printed on a printing press? (*Answer: The Bible in 1456.*)

**Main Course:** There are many "mis-steaks" when it comes to the world of food. Have you ever heard of a London broil steak? Surprisingly, "London broil" is actually the name of a recipe, not a cut of beef. Butchers still mislabel several different beef cuts "London broil." While there are "mis-steaks" all around us, where is one place there are no mistakes? That's right, the Bible!

**Table Talk:**
- What does "All-Scripture is God-breathed" mean?
- The Bible is a complete story from beginning to end. How do you think God accomplished this? What could that one story be?
- Why does it matter to you that God kept His Word free of mistakes?

**Vitamins and Minerals:** "All Scripture is God-breathed and is useful for teaching, rebuking, correcting and training in righteousness, so that the man of God may be thoroughly equipped for every good work" (2 Timothy 3:16–17).

# Mmmmm...Icing on the Cake!

**Mealtime Prayer:** (Tune: "Row, Row, Row Your Boat")
"Thank You, thank You, thank You, Lord,
For the food we eat.
It's so very nice of you
To make some of it sweet!"

**Appetizer:** Did you know that in August 1997, Network Television Marketing Ltd. created a 105-tier cake in Faisalabad, Pakistan? Would you be able to make a cake that big in your kitchen?

Why did the student eat her homework? (*Answer: The teacher told her it was a piece of cake.*)

**Main Course:** Just like a good cake is made up of the finest ingredients, so God's character is made up of only the best. What are some of His "ingredients"? Here are a few to get you started: loving, generous, forgiving. Try to come up with a word to describe God for each letter in your name.

**Table Talk:**
• God is not cake. How can you "taste and see that the LORD is good" (Psalm 34:8)?
• What are some things you will learn when you spend time with God?
• Name three things you can do to be more like God.

**Vitamins and Minerals:** "The LORD our God is righteous in everything he does" (Daniel 9:14).

# Good Grape...Bad Grape...Grape Juice?

**Mealtime Prayer:** Ask God to make you healthy inside and out!

**Appetizer:** In 1869 Dr. Thomas Welch successfully pasteurized Concord grape juice for his church to use in Communion. What color does your tongue turn when you drink grape juice? What other foods make your mouth change colors?

**Main Course:** If you mixed together frozen grape juice and water, would it pour out as spoiled milk? Why not? What's on the inside comes out—whether it's good or bad.
On the outside, Judas looked like one of Jesus' followers, but on the inside he was very different. Read Mark 14:43–46. What seemed to rule in Judas's heart?

Later, Judas realized that no amount of money was worth what he had done. How do you think he felt then?

**Table Talk:**
- Name some desires and thoughts (good or bad), and tell what actions will come out of them.
- How can you get good desires and good thoughts inside?
- Name five things you can buy with a lot of money. How can they lead you away from Jesus?
- What five things that don't cost money can lead you closer to Jesus?

**Vitamins and Minerals:** "Jesus asked him, 'Judas, are you betraying the Son of Man with a kiss?'" (Luke 22:48).

# Wanted: Gifts That VISA® Can't Buy

**Mealtime Prayer:** Ask the Lord to help you find ways to give to people in need, not only to those who can pay you back.

**Appetizer:** Did you know that for $299 you could buy your mom a hand-painted vase from Sweden? Or for $350 you could buy your dad a gold belt buckle? What could your parents buy for you with that much money? What gifts can money not buy?

**Main Course:** Read Luke 10:30–34. What do you think loving others and giving to others mean to Jesus? What is the greatest gift in this story?

Look at the people sitting around the table. Think of a gift that you can give each person without leaving the room. Now, give it. How do you wrap gifts that mean the most?

**Table Talk:**
- What gift did you really appreciate? Why? Who gave it to you?
- What did the Samaritan expect to get back from the man he helped? Why does God ask us to give without expecting anything back?
- Who is one person you might label an "enemy"? What's one thing you could give to or do for him or her?

**Vitamins and Minerals:** "Love your enemies, do good to them, and lend to them without expecting to get anything back" (Luke 6:35).

# Heard WHAT on the Grapevine?

**Mealtime Prayer:** "Lord, just like I'm careful about what goes into my mouth, help me to be careful of what comes out of my mouth. Amen."

**Appetizer:** Place the handle of your fork between your upper lip and your nose. Try holding it there (no hands!) while saying this tongue twister: "Delicious desserts are dandy after dinner."

**Main Course:** Play a game of "Grapevine." Whisper one of the following sentences into the ear of the person to your right. That person has to repeat the sentence to the next person. Continue until the sentence travels around the table. The last person says the sentence out loud. How close was the sentence at the end to the sentence in the beginning?
Sentences:

1. Purple pretzels are the biggest craze among the people of Afghanistan.
2. I don't like popcorn; I like crackers; and my friend Sue likes cheddar cheese.
3. Corn, peas, and milk make an awful drink when they are mixed together.

**Table Talk:**
- Why don't the sentences end the same as they start?
- What happens to gossip when we share it with other people? Why?
- What kinds of things does gossip lead to?
- How can you stop gossip before it starts? When you hear it?

**Vitamins and Minerals:** "Whoever spreads slander is a fool" (Proverbs 10:18).

# No Crying over Spilled Milk

**Mealtime Prayer:** Jesus told us to pray, "Give us today our daily bread. Forgive us our debts, as we also have forgiven our debtors" (Matthew 6:11–12). Set apart a moment to give family members the chance to pray for their meal and ask for forgiveness.

**Appetizer:** Fold a paper towel several times, then drop splotches of food coloring onto it. Open the paper towel to see a colorful pattern. What picture do you see in your pattern?

**Main Course:** In 1938 mothers everywhere rushed to the stores to snatch up a new product. Towels they didn't have to wash! (Better known as paper towels.) Overnight, life became easier. There was no more crying over spilled milk—it could be wiped up in just one swipe! What other things are paper towels used for? But paper towels cannot clean up big messes like the sins in our hearts. Why not? What is the only way to remove the stain of sin?

**Table Talk:**
- Psalm 51:7 says, "Wash me, [Lord,] and I will be whiter than snow." Why won't paper towels do to cleanup your mistakes or "spilled milk"? How does God wash you?
- Give Jesus your "spilled milk." What is it? Ask Him to wash it up.

**Vitamins and Minerals:** "'Come now, let us reason together,' says the Lord. 'Though your sins are like scarlet, they shall be white as snow'" (Isaiah 1:18).

# Wanted: Map Readers and Travelers

**Mealtime Prayer:** The Bible gives us clear directions for prayer. In Matthew 6:9–11, Jesus told us to pray to "our Father in heaven," thanking Him for our "daily bread." Give each family member a chance to do this.

**Appetizer:** Did you know that the Bible has 30,442 verses? If you have memorized verses, say one now.

**Main Course:** Have you ever kept track of your vacation trip on a map? It's exciting to see where you've been, where you are, and where you're going. Name two ways that the Bible is like a map for our lives. Next, read these verses, and then answer the questions.
- Romans 3:23. Where were we before we accepted Jesus? (Stuck in sin.)
- Romans 10:9. Where are we now? (Forgiven in Jesus.)
- 1 Peter 1:3–4. Where are we going? (Heaven.)

**Table Talk:**
- If your best friend lived far away and you had to travel on a journey to his or her house, what five things would you take with you?
- Why can you be excited about the journey the Bible leads you on?
- What other directions does the Bible give to help you on your journey through life?

**Vitamins and Minerals:** "Show me your ways, O LORD, teach me your paths" (Psalm 25:4).

# King on the Mountain

**Mealtime Prayer:** As you thank God for your food, thank Him for the Bible, which teaches us how to live. Ask Him to help you obey His commands.

**Appetizer:** As a family, make up 10 new rules for your house. They can be serious or funny. Put them in order of importance from 1 to 10.

**Main Course:** After Moses led the Israelites across the Red Sea, they traveled through the wilderness and camped by a big mountain. Moses climbed up the mountain to talk to God. God gave Moses laws to tell the people. One day God wrote some rules on two tablets of stone and gave them to Moses. They are known as the Ten Commandments. How many can you name? (See Exodus 20.) Why did God make rules? Why do some people not like rules?

**Table Talk:**
- The first four commandments are about how we relate to God. Why do you think God put those first?
- Why do you think "honor your parents" is right in the middle?
- Why does God want us to obey His commandments?
- What happens when we obey God's commandments?

**Vitamins and Minerals:** [Jesus said,] "If you love me you will obey what I command" (John 14:15).

**FOLLOWING DIRECTIONS/GOD'S WORD/OBEDIENCE**

# A Rocky Ride

**Mealtime Prayer:** Have someone pray the following prayer:
"Dear Lord Jesus, God's only Son,
To You we lift our praise.
Fill our hearts with peace and love
And bless us all our days. Amen."

**Appetizer:** Who are you? Have each person say his or her full name and describe himself or herself with one word. (Example, "My name is James John Jones and I am tall.")
How do you know who people are?

**Main Course:** When Jesus was living on the earth, many people saw Him do amazing things and often wondered who He really was. Read the story in Matthew 8:23–27.
How would you have felt if you were in the boat during the storm? What would you have thought after Jesus calmed it? Why did Jesus have the power to calm the storm?

**Table Talk:**
- Who is Jesus? How do you know?
- What would you say to someone who says, "Jesus was just a good person"?
- Why is it important that Jesus is God? How does it help you in difficult times?

**Vitamins and Minerals:** "Simon Peter answered, 'You are the Christ, the Son of the living God'" (Matthew 16:16).

# The Opposite Game

**Mealtime Prayer:** Ask God to give you wisdom to make the right choices. Thank Him for the wisdom in His Word.

**Appetizer:** Let's play "The Opposite Game." Think of an opposite word for the following words:

| | | | | | |
|---|---|---|---|---|---|
| tall | black | hard | quiet | cold | happy |
| sour | true | rough | in | near | foolish |

**Main Course:** The book of Proverbs has many verses that show how "wise" is the opposite of "foolish." If you were really wise, what could you do? How could you change your world? What are some wise things that people do? What foolish things do people do? Why do they do foolish things? Who do you think is happier, a wise person or a foolish person? Why?

**Table Talk:**
- How can we become wise?
- What should we do if we can't decide whether something is wise or foolish?
- Name three things you need wisdom about. How can you get it?

**Vitamins and Minerals:** "Be very careful . . . how you live—not as unwise but as wise" (Ephesians 5:15).

# Imagine That!

**Mealtime Prayer:** Thank God for creating you in His image so that you can have a relationship with Him.

**Appetizer:** Look at the people sitting around the table. Describe how you are alike and how you are different.

**Main Course:** What are some of the things that God created? How were Adam and Eve different from the rest of creation? Imagine being in a Garden of Eden that God made especially for you. What would your Garden of Eden be like?

**Table Talk:**
- Why do you think God created people in His image? What do you think "in His image" means?
- How are we like God? How are we different from God?
- Why do you think God made such a perfect place for Adam and Eve? What would have been the best thing about it to you? (See Genesis 3:8a.)
- God still provides a "Garden of Eden" for us today. What in your life shows you God cares for you?

**Vitamins and Minerals:** "God created man in his own image, in the image of God he created him; male and female he created them" (Genesis 1:27).

# Construction Zone

**Mealtime Prayer:** Thank God that He is in charge. Ask Him to help us listen to Him and live the way He wants.

**Appetizer:** Guess how many different languages there are today? (*Answer: Over 3000.*) How many can you speak? What would happen if everyone in your family spoke a different language?

**Main Course:** After the Flood, God told Noah's family, "Be fruitful and increase in number and fill the earth" (Genesis 9:1). Why do you think God said that?

Soon there were many more people, but they wanted to stay together instead of "filling the earth." They built a city and a tall tower whose top they hoped would reach to heaven. Why did God not want them to do this?

God made them speak in different languages. How did having different languages force the people to stop building, separate, and scatter the way God wanted them to?

**Table Talk:**
- Do you think people from the same family spoke the same language? Why or why not?
- What was the main thing those people did wrong?
- What happens when we do things our way instead of God's way? What do you need to choose God's way?

**Vitamins and Minerals:** "My word that goes out from my mouth: It will not return to me empty, but will accomplish what I desire and achieve the purpose for which I sent it" (Isaiah 55:11).

# What Time Is It?

**Mealtime Prayer:** Have someone read the following prayer:
"Lord, we thank You for our meal,
For times to laugh and times to heal,
For times to work and times to rest.
Show us, Lord, which way is best. Amen."

**Appetizer:** Have each person tell which of the four seasons he or she likes best and why.

**Main Course:** Ecclesiastes 3:1 says, "There is a time for everything, and a season for every activity under heaven." What are some activities that occur in each season? Why are there times when we laugh and times when we cry? When should we speak and when should we be silent? Why did God create a time for everything?

**Table Talk:**
- How does God know what we need? How does God know our thoughts and feelings?
- How do we know God's timing is perfect?
- Name two things you're waiting to see happen. What helps you wait patiently?

**Vitamins and Minerals:** "He has made everything beautiful in its time. He has also set eternity in the hearts of men; yet they cannot fathom what God has done from beginning to end" (Ecclesiastes 3:11).

# Need Directions?

**Mealtime Prayer:** Thank God for the directions He gives us. Ask Him to help you understand and follow them.

**Appetizer:** Have someone give directions: from home to church; from your house to the nearest park or playground; from sadness to happiness.

**Main Course:** Think of a time when you've been lost. How did you feel? How did you find your way? What happens if we follow the wrong directions? Why is it important to know where we are going? It's important to know where you're going in life, too. Why do we need directions for living?

**Table Talk:**
- Where can we find the right directions for living?
- Why can we trust God's directions?
- What are three of His directions (for example, don't lie)? Name two places you can apply each.

**Vitamins and Minerals:** "Trust in the LORD with all your heart and lean not on your own understanding; in all your ways acknowledge him, and he will make your paths straight" (Proverbs 3:5–6).

# Solve the Mystery

**Mealtime Prayer:** Ask God to help you understand the truth in the Bible.

**Appetizer:** Go to your bookshelf and find a mystery book. Flip it open and read a paragraph. Have people guess what the story is about. Why do some people like reading mysteries while others don't? What is the best part of a mystery? What mysteries would you like answers to?

**Main Course:** Some people think of the Bible as a mystery book because they don't understand what the writers are saying. The prophets often wrote about events that were going to happen in the future. There's a mystery! How did they know about them? (See Hebrews 1:1.)

In the New Testament, the writers spoke of the mystery of the kingdom of heaven. What do you think that means? The apostle Paul says that God has made known the mystery that has been hidden throughout the ages. What is it? (See Colossians 1:27.)

**Table Talk:**
- In some ways, the Bible is like a book with many layers. How does being a Christian help us understand it?
- It's also a book that answers other mysteries, like how to find true happiness. What other mysteries does it explain?
- How does having the mystery explained help you?

**Vitamins and Minerals:** "Oh, the depth of the riches of the wisdom and knowledge of God! How unsearchable his judgments, and his paths beyond tracing out!" (Romans 11:33).

# Bigger Than Big

**Mealtime Prayer:** Praise God for His greatness, for His love, and for His many blessings.

**Appetizer:** What is the biggest thing in the room you're in? In your home? In your town? Who made them? What would you need to know to create things like that?

**Main Course:** God created some mighty big things, like mountains and oceans. What are some other big things God created? What did God need to know to do that? How big do you think God is if He can create those things?

Everything *about* God is big too, like His love and forgiveness. What are some other things about God that are great?

**Table Talk:**
- How would you describe God's greatness to someone who doesn't know Him?
- Name five ways God being great matters or affects how you live (for example, He can help me at school).
- How does God's greatness make you feel safe?

**Vitamins and Minerals:** "Great is the LORD and most worthy of praise; his greatness no one can fathom" (Psalm 145:3).

# Tell Me a Story

**Mealtime Prayer:** Have someone read the following prayer:
"Thank You, Father, for Your Word,
For stories that we've often heard.
Help us learn Your truth today.
Hear us, Father, as we pray. Amen."

**Appetizer:** If you have one ox and someone gives you another ox, what do you have? (*Answer: Parables*—pair of bulls.)

**Main Course:** Jesus was a fantastic storyteller! Many times when Jesus was teaching His disciples or large groups of people, He told interesting stories called parables (see Matthew 13). Why do you think He used stories?

**Table Talk:**
- The parables teach people how God wants them to live and treat one another. How many can you name or tell?
- Do you have a favorite parable? If so, what is it? What does it mean?
- Why do you think Jesus' parables are recorded in the Bible?
- Choose a parable (one you know or one from Matthew 13, 18, or 21:18–22:14). How can it help you improve your relationship?

**Vitamins and Minerals:** "Let me understand the teaching of your precepts; then I will meditate on your wonders" (Psalm 119:27).

# Seeds, Sprouting in a Life near You

**Mealtime Prayer:** "Dear Lord, keep us from being like porridge, slow to boil and hard to stir. Make us like cornflakes: always prepared and ready to serve! Amen."[17]

**Appetizer:** Did you know that archaeologists found seeds in King Tut's tomb? Some seeds were watermelon, wheat, barley, almond, and garlic.[18] What would happen if you planted them? How many sesame seeds are there on a McDonald's Big Mac bun? (*Answer: About 178!*)

**Main Course:** What does a farmer plant when he wants to grow peas? What does he plant when he wants corn? Each plant comes from a unique seed, and within the dry husk lies all the hidden facts about the future plant. What "facts" does a corn kernel know about a corn plant? How are you like that corn seed?

Just as a farmer chooses the seeds he wants, so God chose special characteristics and talents and placed them deep inside you. Close your eyes for a moment and picture the seeds God chose for you.

**Table Talk:**
- What are the special talents God planted deep inside you? How do they tell you who you could be one day?
- What can you do to cultivate your special gifts?
- Name three ways sprouting these gifts can help God's work at your church and at school.

**Vitamins and Minerals:** "We are God's workmanship, created in Christ Jesus to do good works, which God prepared in advance for us to do" (Ephesians 2:10).

[17] Girl Scout Graces: http://www.geocities.com/EnchantedForest/Glade/8851/s8_3.htm
[18] Seed Facts: http://www.huntington.org/BotanicalDiv/Timeline.html

# Daily News: Big Shot Has Big Heart

**Mealtime Prayer:** "O Lord, You are greater than everything and everyone in heaven and earth."

**Appetizer:** Did you know that Andrew Jones of the Atlanta Braves was the youngest player to ever hit a home run in the World Series? He was only 19. If you could break a world record, what would it be?

**Main Course:** Who are your heroes? To the world, these people are "big shots," but men and women of the Bible knew who was responsible for success.

Read Genesis 45:8. Who really made Joseph ruler of all Egypt?

Read Esther 4:14. Why was Esther placed in the palace? By whom?

Read 1 Timothy 2:7. Why was Paul raised up as a teacher? Who gave him that position?

It's fine to appreciate talents and honor and to respect people who have been especially blessed. But why should we not think of others or ourselves as "big shots"? To God, are some people more important than others? Why or why not?

**Table Talk:**
- Name three people you've thought to be more important than you are. Are they really?
- Who is the only true Big Shot?
- Why is it good to let others know who helped us succeed?

**Vitamins and Minerals:** "Many are the plans in a man's heart, but it is the LORD's purpose that prevails" (Proverbs 19:21).

# Believe It or Not: Sometimes Little Is More

**Mealtime Prayer:** Ask God to help you give to others things that matter to you, things that cost.

**Appetizer:** Fill a small cup with warm water. Put a couple swallows of a favorite drink in a large cup. (Make sure the cups aren't see-through.) Hold them up, and ask your children which they'd rather have. After they choose, show them the inside of the cups. Why did they choose the one they did? How did they feel when they first saw the amounts? Which tasted better?

**Main Course:** What matters more, amount or content? What would mean more: If a person with a truckload of cookies offered you one cookie, or if a friend who had only one cookie gave it to you? Why?

A similar thing happened in the Bible. Read Mark 12:41–44.

**Table Talk:**
- Why was the widow's coin worth more than what the others gave? Why do you think she gave it all?
- If you gave your last coin away like she did, how would you survive? Where would you place your trust?
- What stops you from giving sometimes?
- What can you give today? Who can you give it to?

**Vitamins and Minerals:** "They all gave out of their wealth; but she, out of her poverty, put in everything—all she had to live on" (Mark 12:44).

**GIVING/SACRIFICE**

# "Lettuce" Pray

**Mealtime Prayer:**
"We thank You, Father, for our evening meal,
For fun and friends and the joy we feel.
For blessing and guidance and love we pray.
Be with us now and each new day. Amen."

**Appetizer:** Did you know that lettuce is a member of the sunflower family? One kind of lettuce was called "Crisphead" until the 1920s. It was renamed "Iceberg" when California began transporting lettuce underneath mounds of ice to keep it cool. Can you think of four other foods that need to be kept cold while they're being transported to stores?

**Main Course:** If you had to make "Lettuce Pray Salad," what ingredients would you need? Thankfulness and confession are two possibilities. Come up with two more. How could you serve this to your God?

Make your own salad: On construction paper (preferably green), have each person write his or her own prayer. Use different ingredients you thought up. Toss these prayers in a bowl, and then lift the bowl heavenward as a sign of your family offering prayers to God.

**Table Talk:**
- Why does God enjoy a "salad" like this?
- What else could you add to this type of salad?

**Vitamins and Minerals:** "Pray in the Spirit on all occasions with all kinds of prayers and requests" (Ephesians 6:18).

# Fresh-Baked "Roll" Models

**Mealtime Prayer:** Jesus prayed that the world would know the love of God (John 17:23). This is a good example to follow. After you pray for your meal, pray that the world can see God's love through your family.

**Appetizer:** Did you know that the proper etiquette for eating rolls is to break them in half or in small pieces before buttering and eating them? What are two other table rules?

**Main Course:** Have you ever had someone say, "I could tell right away that you were part of that family"? What might give you away? Even if you don't look like anyone else in your family, perhaps you walk like your father or talk like your mother. Why?

How are your parents your role models? What other people are role models in your life? How can we distinguish between good role models and bad ones?

**Table Talk:**
- Why was Jesus the perfect role model? Why did He tell His disciples to copy Him in all things?
- In what ways did He show us how to love?
- What about you helps others recognize that you are part of God's family?

**Vitamins and Minerals:** "As I have loved you, so you must love one another. By this all men will know that you are my disciples, if you love one another" (John 13:34–35).

# Simon Says—God Says!

**Mealtime Prayer:** God says that we should pray for each other (Ephesians 6:18). Take time to do this after thanking God for your food.

**Appetizer:** Did you know that because people obey God and tell others about Jesus, the Bible has been translated into over 1,946 languages? If you could learn another language, which would you choose?

**Main Course:** Play a game of "Simon Says," giving everyone an opportunity to be Simon. If someone completes the action without the leader saying "Simon Says," that person is out until a new leader takes over.

The Bible gives us instructions too. Think of it as "God Says." God tells us what we should do when we're sitting, walking, and lying down. It doesn't matter what we're doing, we should always think about what God says!

**Table Talk:**
- What was your favorite instruction in "Simon Says"? What was the most difficult to follow?
- What is your favorite Bible instruction? What is the most difficult to follow?
- What happens when you don't obey what God says? (Remember that God is faithful to forgive!) How can you check what you're doing with what "God says"?

**Vitamins and Minerals:** "Fix these words of mine in your hearts and minds. . . . [Talk] about them when you sit at home and when you walk along the road, when you lie down and when you get up" (Deuteronomy 11:18–19).

**GAMES/INSTRUCTIONS/OBEDIENCE/THE BIBLE**

# Weather Forecast: Heavenly Sunshine

**Mealtime Prayer:** "Dear Lord, shine Your love upon this table and on every heart present. Amen."

**Appetizer:** What kind of days do you feel your best, sunny days or cloudy days? Did you know that along with food and exercise, sunshine is needed to make you healthy? In fact, people who don't get enough sun get a disease called rickets. How do you feel when you don't get enough sun?

**Main Course:** What do you think Jesus looks like? Read Revelation 1:13–16 for a description of how the apostle John saw Jesus. How is your idea of Jesus different from the one John saw? How does this image of Jesus show His power and glory?

The Bible says, "The LORD God is a sun" (Psalm 84:11). How has He been your "sunshine" today?

**Table Talk:**
- What parts of God's character help you feel better?
- How are God and the sun similar? (Example: The sun warms our bodies; God warms our hearts with His love.)
- Which is greater, God's sun or God's Son? Why?
- How can the sun remind you of God's presence this week?

**Vitamins and Minerals:** "The LORD God is a sun and shield" (Psalm 84:11).

# Not Hanging with the Crowd

**Mealtime Prayer:** "Lord, I'd rather be like broccoli and stand up for You than be like chocolate and melt when the heat is on."

**Appetizer:** What is the most unusual food you can think of? What is the most unusual animal? Have you ever been the only kid at the lunch table eating carrot sticks while everyone else is chomping fruity snack cakes? Why can it be hard being unusual?

**Main Course:** Did you know that God calls us to be different than non-Christians? In what ways? Moses was a Hebrew baby adopted by Pharaoh's daughter. He could have spent his days living in riches, but what did he do instead? (Read Hebrews 11:23–25).

When God asked Moses to take the Hebrews out of Egypt, did Moses let his nervousness about being different stop him? (Read Exodus 4:18; 5:1–2.)

Hebrews 11:27 says, "[Moses] persevered because he saw him who is invisible." Who is that invisible person?

**Table Talk:**
- When is one time you were forced to be different? How did you feel? How did God help you?
- What can be really good about being different? What three things that make you different can you be thankful for?

**Vitamins and Minerals:** "Obey me, and I will be your God and you will be my people. Walk in all the ways I command you, that it may go well with you" (Jeremiah 7:23).

# No More Baby Food!

**Mealtime Prayer:** Ask the Lord to help you to crave His Word as much as you crave food for your body.

**Appetizer:** Hide the meal and instead serve milk, crackers, and applesauce. Note your family's reaction. Ask your family, "Would you be satisfied with this meal? Why or why not?" Bring out the real meal and talk about the difference between the two.

**Main Course:** Read Hebrews 5:12–14. When it comes to God's Word, why are some people content with "baby food" beliefs? Why are "baby food" beliefs easier to handle and "digest"? What "solid food" is for believers? How do you think believers can move on to solid food? What do you have to be aware of to move on to "solid food"? (The difference between good and evil.)

**Table Talk:**
- What would you be like if you only ate baby food?
- What was one thing today that seemed evil to you? What was one thing that seemed good? How did you know the difference?
- How will studying the Bible help you "grow up" in your faith?

**Vitamins and Minerals:** "Solid food is for the mature, who by constant use have trained themselves to distinguish good from evil" (Hebrews 5:14).

# Native American Thanks

**Mealtime Prayer:**

| | |
|---|---|
| "Eagles thank God for the mountains. | *(Flap arms like wings.)* |
| Fish thank God for the sea. | *(Put hands together like a swimming fish.)* |
| We thank God for our blessings, | *(Bow heads, fold hands.)* |
| For what we're about to receive." | *(Open hands toward dinner table.)* |

**Appetizer:** Pumpkins, zucchini, sweet potatoes, turkey, peanuts, and maple syrup are all of Native American origin. What foods are you most thankful for?

"Texas" is a Native American word that means "friend." There are also 25 other U.S. states derived from Native American names. Guess which ones. What do you appreciate most about the place where you live? How can you thank God for that?

**Main Course:** Create a special centerpiece for your table. Have each family member choose one item to represent something he or she is thankful for. (For example, a clothespin can represent the clothing God provides for your family.) Each say a simple prayer of thanks as you place your items on the table.

**Table Talk:**
- Why is it important to say "thank you" throughout the year?
- If you had to say "thank you" without words, what would it look like?
- How does saying "thank you" change *you*?

**Vitamins and Minerals:** "Give thanks to the LORD, call on his name; make known among the nations what he has done" (Psalm 105:1).

# Who Said It?

**Mealtime Prayer:** Thank God for the messages He gives us in the Bible and for His messengers.

**Appetizer:** Let's play some "Who Said It?" Bible trivia:

Q: Who told Pharaoh there was going to be a famine in Egypt? (*Answer: Joseph.*)

Q: Who was sent to preach God's Word to the people of Nineveh? (*Answer: Jonah.*)

Q: Who told Mary she was going to have a baby who would be the Messiah? (*Answer: The angel Gabriel.*)

**Main Course:** Have you ever had to deliver a message? Who was the message for? What was it? Why was it important to get the message right?

In the Bible, God often used messengers to deliver messages for Him. How many can you think of? Sometimes He used people, sometimes He used angels, and one time He even used a donkey! What are some messages that you've read in the Bible? How are they useful for us today?

**Table Talk:**

- What should you do with God's message? If you were to send a reply, what would it say?
- What or who are some of God's messengers today?
- Name three messages from God that you can give to others.

**Vitamins and Minerals:** "I did not speak of my own accord, but the Father who sent me commanded me what to say and how to say it" (John 12:49).

# Prune Face

**Mealtime Prayer:** Thank God for His goodness, His mercy, and His forgiveness. Ask Him to help you forgive those who have offended you.

**Appetizer:** Place a plum and a prune on a plate. How are they alike? How are they different? Did you know that a prune is a shriveled-up plum? How do you think a plum turns into a prune?

**Main Course:** Have one person smile while another person frowns. How are their faces different? How is a smiling face like a plum? How is a frowning face like a prune? Which do you prefer to look at? Why?

Some people who are angry walk around with shriveled-up prune faces. God doesn't like it when we walk around angry. The Bible tells us to get rid of our anger on the very same day that we become angry. How can we get rid of anger and turn from a prune to a plum?

**Table Talk:**
- Forgiveness is a key to losing anger and gaining joy. Why should we forgive others? How do we do that?
- Why does God forgive us when we sin?
- Would you rather be a prune face or a plum face? How can you help each other do that?

**Vitamins and Minerals:** "'In your anger do not sin': Do not let the sun go down while you are still angry" (Ephesians 4:26).

# Truth or Consequences

**Mealtime Prayer:** Have someone say the following prayer:
"Lord, we thank You for Your Word,
We know Your Word is true.
Help us to obey Your Word
In everything we do. Amen."

**Appetizer:** Play a game of "Truth or Consequences." Divide the family into two teams. Have each team make up five true or false questions about anything you can think of. Have the teams take turns asking the questions. The team that gets the most correct answers wins. The other team has to do the dishes!

**Main Course:** Think of some of the excuses you have heard. What was the strangest one that was true? How do you know it was true?

Think of some lies you've heard or told. How was it discovered that they were lies? What happened?

**Table Talk:**
- What is the difference between the consequences of telling the truth and telling lies? Why do you think that is so?
- Why is truth the best policy?
- Where or when is it hard for you to tell the truth? What can help you be honest?

**Vitamins and Minerals:** "A false witness will not go unpunished, and he who pours out lies will not go free" (Proverbs 19:5).

**GOD'S WORD/TRUTH**

# Give Me a Break

**Mealtime Prayer:** Thank God that He loves us and cares about us, and that He wants to help us with our problems.

**Appetizer:** Here are some "problems" to figure out:
    Q: What is black and white and has 16 wheels? (*Answer: A zebra on roller skates*.)
    Q: What do you call a mosquito with a tin suit? (*Answer: A bite in shining armour*.)
Can you think of others?

**Main Course:** Here are some possible problems: bad hair day; science class; how to get the last drop out of the Coke can; your friend is angry with you. What two problems do you face? Come up with a solution for each, such as "Wet your hair and start again." Some problems are harder to solve. Where can you go for help?

    The Bible tells us that God loves us and cares about our problems. First Peter 5:7 says, "Cast all your anxiety on him because he cares for you." What does that mean?

**Table Talk:**
- Why can God help you find the solution to any problem? Why will He?
- How do we give our problems to God?
- How does doing that help us feel better?
- Name two ways you can discover God's answer to your problems.

**Vitamins and Minerals:** "Come to me, all you who are weary and burdened, and I will give you rest" (Matthew 11:28).

# Boy, Oh, Boy!

**Mealtime Prayer:** Think of a time when God answered a specific prayer. Thank Him for answering your prayers.

**Appetizer:** Have each person say his or her name and tell its meaning. If you don't know what your name means, what would you like it to mean? Why? Does the meaning of your name describe who you are as a person? Why or why not?

**Main Course:** Have you ever wanted something so badly that it was all you could think about? What was it? Did you get it?

There was a woman in the Bible named Hannah who didn't have any children. She wanted a son so badly that it was all she could think about. Every day she prayed for a son until God finally answered her prayer. Hannah named her baby boy Samuel, which means "name of God." Why do you think God answered Hannah's prayer? Why do you think Hannah named her baby Samuel?

**Table Talk:**
- Is it okay to ask God for something we want badly? Why or why not?
- What's more important, telling God what you want or getting what you want? Why?
- What should we do if we don't get what we ask for?
- Why does God want us to pray?

**Vitamins and Minerals:** "Delight yourself in the LORD and he will give you the desires of your heart" (Psalm 37:4).

# Back to the Cradle

**Mealtime Prayer:** Thank God for sending His Son into the world to save us from our sins.

**Appetizer:** Get out family baby pictures ahead of time and bring them to the table. Ask:
Q: When were you born?
Q: Where were you born?
Q: What did you weigh at birth?

**Main Course:** Tell each child one special thing about when he or she was a baby. Why are babies so special? Why do they need to be cared for? What would happen if babies did not grow up?

There was a man in the Bible named Nicodemus who was talking to Jesus one night. Jesus told him he had to be born again in order to see the kingdom of God. Nicodemus was very confused. He thought he had to become a baby again (John 3:1–6). What do you think Jesus meant?

**Table Talk:**
- How is becoming a Christian like being a baby?
- How can new Christians grow spiritually?
- When do Christians stop growing? When *should* they stop?
- How old are you spiritually? Compare that to physical ages. What would you be? A newborn? A toddler? A teenager? Why?

**Vitamins and Minerals:** "Believe in the Lord Jesus, and you will be saved" (Acts 16:31).

# Be a Peach

**Mealtime Prayer:**
"Heavenly Father up above, Fill us with Your peace and love.
Help us to be kind and good And do the things we know we should.
Thank You for our food today. Hear us, Father, as we pray. Amen."

**Appetizer:** Gather as many different kinds of fruit as you can and place them on the table. For each type of fruit, think of positive character traits that begin with the same letter (for example, peach: pleasant, polite).

**Main Course:** If you could be any kind of fruit tree, what would you be? Why?
The Bible says that Christians are like trees that bear fruit. The "fruit" we bear, however, isn't the fruit we eat, like apples or bananas. God's Spirit in us helps us bear His fruit (see the Vitamins and Minerals). It's seen in the way we act and how we treat others. What kinds of "fruit" are growing in your house?

**Table Talk:**
• What kind of "fruit" do you want to grow on your "tree"? How can you help it grow?
• Why does God care about how we act and treat other people?
• What kind of "fertilizer" or "pruning" would help your "tree" produce good fruit?

**Vitamins and Minerals:** "The fruit of the Spirit is love, joy, peace, patience, kindness, goodness, faithfulness, gentleness and self-control. Against such things there is no law" (Galatians 5:22–23).

# I Spy!

**Mealtime Prayer:** Think about some of the wonderful things that God has created for you to enjoy every day. Thank Him for those things when you pray.

**Appetizer:** Count how many living things (bigger than your thumbnail) are in your house, including plants and pets. Guess how many different kinds of trees and animals there are in the world. (*Answer: There are more than 60,000 kinds of trees, and over one million kinds of animals!*)

**Main Course:** Look at the food on your plate and the items on the table. Look at the floor, the ceiling, and everything in between. Look at the people sitting around the table. Look out a window or walk outside. Ready? Now take turns sharing one thing you noticed that is a part of God's creation, and tell how it is good for you. (For example, water is healthy for our bodies and helps plants and trees to grow.) Keep taking turns until everyone shares what he or she has found.

**Table Talk:**
- Why do you think God created so many different things? What could their purpose be?
- What does God want us to do with what He made?
- Why do you think God created you?

**Vitamins and Minerals:** "God saw all that he had made, and it was very good" (Genesis 1:31).

# Be a Wise Guy

**Mealtime Prayer:** As you thank God for His blessings, ask Him to bless you with the gift of wisdom.

**Appetizer:** Read Proverbs 1:8, then make up a proverb together as a family. (For example, he who eats vegetables gets dessert.)

**Main Course:** If you could have anything in the world, what would you ask for and why? God told King Solomon he could have anything he wanted. Do you know what Solomon asked for? (He asked for wisdom.) Why do you think King Solomon asked for that? The Bible tells us that King Solomon was wiser than any other man (1 Kings 4:31). How could wisdom be helpful to a king? How can wisdom help us in our everyday lives?

**Table Talk:**
- Name some situations where you could use wisdom (for example, when a classmate asks you to give her the answer). How can you get that wisdom?
- Just having wisdom isn't enough. You have to use it. What would you do with your wisdom when you got it? (For example, would you say no, tell the teacher, or pray for your friend?)

**Vitamins and Minerals:** "If any of you lacks wisdom, he should ask God, who gives generously to all without finding fault, and it will be given to him" (James 1:5).

# What's New?

**Mealtime Prayer:** Thank God for His never-ending love, His faithfulness, and His forgiveness.

**Appetizer:** After everyone finds his or her place at the table, get up and have everyone switch places. How do you feel sitting in a different place?

**Main Course:** If you could change two things about your life, what would they be?

Did you ever have a best friend who found a new best friend or who moved away?

Did you ever look forward to being with someone, and then that person changed his or her plans? How did you feel? Why are some changes bad?

Name some changes that could happen in your life. When can changes be good? When can staying the same be good? When can it be bad?

With God, things never change. The Bible tells us He is always the same.

**Table Talk:**
- What are some things about God that you hope will never change?
- How does the fact that God never changes make you feel?
- How would our lives be different if God changed from day to day?
- Our lives change. What are some positive ways to handle changes or disappointments?

**Vitamins and Minerals:** "Jesus Christ is the same yesterday and today and forever" (Hebrews 13:8).

# Salt of the Earth

**Mealtime Prayer:** (Tune: "Zip-a-Dee-Doo-Dah")
   "Zip-a-dee-do-dah, zip-a-dee-ay,
   We are grateful for Your blessings today.
   Here at God's table, love's everywhere.
   Let us be salt, with good things to share!"

**Appetizer:** Did you know that Roman soldiers were given a salt allowance, or *salarium*? This is where our word *salary* comes from. If you had to work for a salary, what job would you choose?

**Main Course:** Salt has military importance. Thousands of Napoleon's troops died when their wounds would not heal because of a lack of salt. Also, in 1777, during the Revolutionary War, the British Lord Howe was jubilant when he succeeded in capturing General Washington's salt supply.

   Salt is very important. It keeps our bodies balanced and our blood stable. It preserves food and adds flavor. It also makes us thirsty . . . and just one handful of salt goes a long way.

**Table Talk:**
   • Jesus called His believers "salt of the earth." How are Christians like salt?
   • How do we bring stability? Preserve goodness? Add flavor?
   • How do believers help others thirst for God? How does a handful of us go a long way?
   • Name one way you can be salt to those around you today.

**Vitamins and Minerals:** "You are the salt of the earth" (Matthew 5:13).

# Menu Item: Tastes Like Chicken

**Mealtime Prayer:** Jesus often prayed alone (Matthew 14:23). Have each person pray silently for their food.

**Appetizer:** Have you heard that frog legs taste just like chicken? Have you ever eaten frog? If so, have you personally found this to be true? Frogs may taste that way, but a chicken is a chicken and a frog is a frog! What are three differences between the two?

**Main Course:** People sometimes confuse other things. Have you heard someone say, "The Bible has good stories, but I don't believe they have anything to do with real life"? How would you respond? What Bible verses could you use to show that person the truth? (2 Timothy 3:15–17 is one reference. Can you think of another?)

The Bible is like an instruction manual for life. What does that mean?

**Table Talk:**
- Why is it important to make a habit of reading God's Instruction Manual? What time could you set aside each day to do this?
- How can praying before you read the Bible help?
- Why does studying God's Word help you know the difference between the real thing and poor substitutes?

**Vitamins and Minerals:** "Do your best to present yourself to God as one approved, a workman who does not need to be ashamed and who correctly handles the word of truth" (2 Timothy 2:15).

# God Is "Berry" Good!

**Mealtime Prayer:** "Lord, I pray today that at this meal we shall fellowship with You. Amen."

**Appetizer:**
Q: When does 1 + 1 + 1 = 1?
*A: When Father + Son + Holy Spirit = God.*

**Main Course:** To show an example of the Trinity, bring out a fruit pie. Slice the pie into three pieces. Point out how the three pieces are separate but are all part of the whole. The insides may run together, but they are still different pieces. How is this pie like God? (The Father, Son, and Holy Spirit are three-in-one!)

**Table Talk:**
- Read Luke 10:21. What is one of the Father's roles?
- Read John 14:26. What is one of the Holy Spirit's roles?
- Read John 3:16–17. What is Jesus' main role?
- Why are all these roles needed?
- How does each Person of the Trinity help you in daily living?

**Vitamins and Minerals:** "Make disciples of all nations, baptizing them in the name of the Father and of the Son and of the Holy Spirit" (Matthew 28:19).

# Heavenly Preparations in Progress

**Mealtime Prayer:** Close your eyes and imagine a meal set before you in heaven. Thank God for the food He's given you today and the food He's preparing for you in heaven.

**Appetizer:** Did you know that truffles are a small fungus that grows close to the roots of trees in woodlands? They are hunted with dogs and hogs, which are able to scent them out underground, and they sell for more than $300 a pound wholesale! How do you think even expensive truffles would compare to food in heaven?

**Main Course:** Thomas was a follower of Jesus. He was sad to hear that Jesus was leaving and wanted to know how to follow Him. Read John 14:2–6. Where was Jesus going? What was He going to do?

**Table Talk:**
- From what Jesus told Thomas, who is "the way" to heaven? What does that mean?
- What does it mean that Jesus is "the truth"?
- What does it mean that Jesus is "the life"?
- In your own words, how would you describe heaven? What special preparations do you think Jesus is making for you there?

**Vitamins and Minerals:** "Jesus replied, 'Where I am going, you cannot follow now, but you will follow later'" (John 13:36).

# Adam's Apple

**Mealtime Prayer:** "Lord, help me to be content with the fact that You will never leave me nor forsake me."

**Appetizer:**
Q: At what time of the day did God create Adam?
*A: A little before Eve.*

**Main Course:** On your body, where is your Adam's apple located? Your Adam's apple is part of your voice box, but it's different from Adam's "apple" (or fruit) in the Bible. Read Genesis 2:17 and Genesis 3:4–5. What did God say would happen if Adam ate from the Tree of the Knowledge of Good and Evil? What was different about what the serpent told Eve? Who was right?

Satan was tricky. He tempted Eve by making her think she was missing out on something special and that God was wrong. Where does Satan's way always lead?

**Table Talk:**
- What things does Satan make you feel you're missing out on? How does he try to convince you God is wrong? What happens when you believe him?
- What can you do when Satan tempts you?

**Vitamins and Minerals:** "I have learned the secret of being content" (Philippians 4:12).

# PB&J (Peanut Butter & Jelly?)

**Mealtime Prayer:** Look around the table at all the goodness God has provided. Praise the Lord for those things.

**Appetizer:** Read Psalm 148:1–5. Give each family member a special word or phrase to shout, such as "Amen," "I believe," or "Joy," every time you read the word "praise." If you like, have him or her lift their hands as they shout.

**Main Course:** Have you ever had one of those difficult days when nothing seems to go right? Try a PB&J. Not a peanut butter and jelly sandwich—praise, belief, and joy. Name three ways these three things can change your day.

**Table Talk:**
- What things has God done that you can praise Him for (for example, made it possible to have ice cream)? Why does God deserve to be praised?
- Why do you believe that God hears your prayers? What other things do you believe about God (for example, He loves you)?
- What things God put in your life give you joy? How does having a relationship with God bring you joy?

**Vitamins and Minerals:** "I will praise you as long as I live, and in your name I will lift up my hands" (Psalm 63:4).

# Tomato Face!

**Mealtime Prayer:** Do you have a tendency to get into trouble? Tonight, as you thank God for your food, also ask Him to help you be obedient.

**Appetizer:** Did you know that when tomatoes were first brought to Europe from the New World in the sixteenth century some people believed they brought good luck, so they made stuffed fabric pincushions to look like them?[19] Tomatoes don't really bring good luck, but they are useful for other things. Name a few.

**Main Course:** What kinds of things give you a "tomato" (red) face? For example, have you ever gotten into trouble in front of your friends? Did your face turn bright red like a tomato? All of us mess up once in a while, but God can help. Repentance means turning away from sin, toward obedience. How can you do that? Is there anything you need to turn from?

**Table Talk:**
- What does God do when we repent? How does that feel?
- How can reading the Bible help us to stay out of trouble?
- Read Proverbs 11:17; 19:23; and 28:14. How is that type of help sure to keep your face from turning red?

**Vitamins and Minerals:** "Is any one of you in trouble? He should pray. Is anyone happy? Let him sing songs of praise" (James 5:13).

[19] Ethnic Food Web site: http://www.eatethnic.com/FunFacts.htm

# Don't Go Solo

**Mealtime Prayer:** Thank God for each person at your table. Ask Him to show you ways to work together as one.

**Appetizer:** Look around. What work needs to be done around your house tonight? Does the kitchen need to be cleaned? Does the yard need to be raked? How can those chores become fun? After the meal, instead of "going solo," pick one chore and tackle it as a team. Pay attention to how quickly the work gets done and how much fun you'll have together!

**Main Course:** What does "solo" mean? Even though Jesus was all-powerful, He didn't go solo. He called 12 men to help Him in His work and called them His disciples. What did Jesus do for His disciples? How did those disciples help Jesus?

Those men, and all the believers who followed, were part of God's plan. No going solo in God's kingdom!

**Table Talk:**
- What are some ways we can be part of God's team (for example, help others)?
- Jesus prayed, "Holy father, protect them . . . so that they may be one as we are one" (John 17:11). What do you think He meant? How can we be one (be close and at peace) with other people?
- What kinds of things keep us from being one with others?

**Vitamins and Minerals:** "Encourage one another daily, as long as it is called Today" (Hebrews 3:13).

**BODY OF CHRIST/WORKING TOGETHER**

# Gigantic, Enormous Grocery List

**Mealtime Prayer:** "Thank You, O Lord, for this food. May we always have faith that You will provide. Amen."

**Appetizer:** Did you know that in one year an average zoo elephant eats 1,600 loaves of bread, 2,000 potatoes, 1,500 gallons of mixed grains, 100,000 pounds of hay, 12,000 pounds of dried alfalfa, and 3,000 other vegetables?[20] How long would it take for you to eat that much food (except for the hay!)?

**Main Course:** Have you ever helped make a grocery list? What things did it include? Read Genesis 6:17–22. What do you think Noah's grocery list looked like for the ark? (Read Genesis 9:2–3.) With God's help, Noah built the ark and gathered the food for his family and the animals. How does God help your parents gather (buy) food for your zoo—uh, family?

**Table Talk:**
- No one had seen rain before the Flood, and Noah didn't live near water. What would the neighbors have thought of his boat building? Why do you think Noah kept going?
- How is Noah's obedience an example of faith?
- What if Noah hadn't done all God commanded? What might have happened?
- God might not ask you to build a boat or save the world, but what could happen if you disobeyed Him?

**Vitamins and Minerals:** "By faith Noah, when warned about things not yet seen, in holy fear built an ark to save his family" (Hebrews 11:7).

[20] *Zoobooks*, "Elephants" (San Diego: Wildlife Education, leaflet).

# Choices, Choices

**Mealtime Prayer:** Sometimes prayer is asking for help. Ask God to help you choose what is right.

**Appetizer:** Place a piece of candy under one of three overturned cups. Mix them up, then tell your children to choose a cup. How did wanting that candy help you choose? Would you make the same choice if a spider was under the cup? Why or why not?

**Main Course:** After Moses died, Joshua led the people to the Promised Land. But they soon picked up bad habits from their neighbors. Joshua told them, "'[God] gave you a land on which you did not toil and cities you did not build; and you live in them and eat from vineyards and olive groves that you did not plant.' . . . But if serving the LORD seems undesirable to you, then choose for yourselves this day whom you will serve. . . . But as for me and my household, we will serve the LORD" (Joshua 24:13–15).

What difference would their choice make? Should this have been a difficult choice? What things keep us from choosing God?

**Table Talk:**
- What was the simplest choice you made today? The most difficult?
- If Joshua asked you his question, what would you choose? Why?
- Have you ever had to choose God's ways over the ways of a group? What happened?

**Vitamins and Minerals:** "I have chosen the way of truth" (Psalm 119:30).

# When Life Is the Pits

**Mealtime Prayer:** Ask God to give you patience and to trust Him during difficult times.

**Appetizer:** Have everyone taste a spoon of cottage cheese. How does it taste? It may taste bad, but guess what? Cottage cheese is actually good for you. It's full of nutrients and proteins.

**Main Course:** Think of a time when you thought something was going to be bad for you but it turned out to be good. What happened? What did you learn?

The Bible tells of a boy named Joseph who was thrown into a pit by his brothers and later sold as a slave and taken to Egypt. What do you think Joseph thought about that? How would you have responded? How did this bad thing become good? (See Genesis 41.)

Joseph trusted God and kept on doing what was right. When his brothers came to Egypt to get food, they were afraid of Joseph. But Joseph wasn't mad. He said, "You intended to harm me, but God intended it for good" (Genesis 50:20).

**Table Talk:**
- When things don't go the way we want them to, how do you feel? How easy is it to trust that God loves you right then?
- What can help you trust God's love in those times?
- Name two ways you can be like Joseph.

**Vitamins and Minerals:** "We know that in all things God works for the good of those who love him, who have been called according to his purpose" (Romans 8:28).

# God's Telephone Number

**Mealtime Prayer:** "Our Father who art in heaven, hallowed be thy name. Thy kingdom come, thy will be done, on earth as it is in heaven. Give us this day our daily bread. Forgive us our debts as we have forgiven our debtors. And lead us not into temptation, but deliver us from evil. For Thine is the kingdom and the power and the glory forever. Amen."

**Appetizer:** Have one person think of a short message such as "Eat all your vegetables" or "Baseball is a great sport." Without using words, try to get the others to understand the message.

**Main Course:** What are the many different ways we can talk to our friends and relatives? Which form of communication do you like best? What can you do if you don't know someone's telephone number? How can you get God's "telephone" number? Jeremiah 33:3 says, "Call to me and I will answer you."

**Table Talk:**
- What different ways can you talk to God? What kinds of things should we include in our prayers?
- When can we pray?
- How can God hear more than one prayer at the same time?
- How does God communicate with you?

**Vitamins and Minerals:** "Pray in the Spirit on all occasions with all kinds of prayers and requests" (Ephesians 6:18).

# Giant Grapes

**Mealtime Prayer:** As you thank God for your food, have each person give thanks to God for a specific blessing he or she is grateful for.

**Appetizer:** Using the word "blessings," think of one or two blessings that begin with each letter. For example, b=bread, l=liver (liver?) . . .

**Main Course:** Moses sent 12 spies into the Promised Land of Canaan to check it out. Joshua and Caleb were excited to see the giant grapes and rich, fertile land. But the other spies were afraid because the people were so big. "We can't attack those people," they said (Numbers 13:31). But Joshua and Caleb said, "If the LORD is pleased with us, he will lead us into the land, a land flowing with milk and honey, and will give it to us" (14:8). Why do you think Joshua and Caleb had a different report than the rest of the spies? If you were one of the spies, would you have been afraid of the giant people, or excited about the giant grapes? Why?

**Table Talk:**
- What blessings (like peace or confidence) can we enjoy if we trust in God?
- What "giants" do you have in your life? (Math? A bully?) What are you doing about them?
- What "grapes" (like a best friend) do you have in your life? Thank God for them.

**Vitamins and Minerals:** "Taste and see that the LORD is good; blessed is the man who takes refuge in him" (Psalm 34:8).

# Talking Stones

**Mealtime Prayer:** Think of times when you've seen God's power in your life. Thank Him for those times.

**Appetizer:** How long is the Jordan River from north to south? Take a wild guess! (*Answer: About two hundred miles long.*)

**Main Course:** After Moses died, Joshua was chosen to lead the Israelites across the Jordan River and into the Promised Land. If you had to lead your family across a river, how would you do it? What would you need? Read the exciting story of how Joshua did it in Joshua 3:14–4:7.

**Table Talk:**
- Why do you think God told Joshua to set up the memorial?
- Why is it important to remember what God does for us?
- What memorials do we have in our home (for example, a wedding album)? What do they remind you of?

**Vitamins and Minerals:** "[God] did this so that all the peoples of the earth might know that the hand of the LORD is powerful and so that you might always fear the LORD your God" (Joshua 4:24).

# Bite Your Tongue!

**Mealtime Prayer:** Ask God to help you speak words that are pleasing to Him and kind to others.

**Appetizer:** Did you know that the tongue has over 10,000 taste buds that are grouped into four categories? The taste buds in the front help you taste sweet flavors. The taste buds on the sides taste sour and salty food. The ones in the back taste bitter flavors. Why is this arrangement good when it comes to licking an ice-cream cone?

**Main Course:** What does it feel like to bite your tongue? Have you ever heard the saying "Bite your tongue"? What does that mean? When is it best to "bite our tongues"? What could happen if we say something we shouldn't? What should we do if we've said something that hurt someone else?

**Table Talk:**
- Why is it important for us to control our tongues? Why is it hard?
- Come up with two sayings that can help you learn to control them.
- How do our words affect others? Why does God care what we say to them?

**Vitamins and Minerals:** "I have worthy things to say; I open my lips to speak what is right" (Proverbs 8:6).

# All in the Family

**Mealtime Prayer:** Thank God for all the members in your family. Thank Him also that you are a part of His family.

**Appetizer:** If you gave a party for all of your aunts, uncles, cousins, and grandparents, what would it be like and what would you do?

**Main Course:** What does the word *family* mean? What are some of the benefits of being in a family? What are some of the responsibilities? How are the people in your family the same? How are they different?

God's family is like yours in some ways. Who is in it? How does a person join up? How are the people in God's family the same? How are they different?

**Table Talk:**
- Why would you want to be part of God's family? What responsibilities or "chores" does it have? What good things does it bring?
- Why does God want people to join His family?
- How can you help to get more people into God's family?

**Vitamins and Minerals:** "You are no longer foreigners and aliens, but fellow citizens with God's people and members of God's household" (Ephesians 2:19).

# A Garden of Goodness

**Mealtime Prayer:**
"For rosy apples, juicy plums, and yellow pears so sweet,
For hips and haws and bush and hedge, and flowers at our feet,
For ears of corn all ripe and dry, and colored leaves on trees,
We thank You, heavenly Father God, for such good gifts as these."
—*Author unknown*[21]

**Appetizer:** Did you know that onions, garlic, and asparagus are lilies; the sweet potato is a morning glory; and peanuts are beans, not nuts?[22] What other things are not what they seem?

**Main Course:** What do people know you by? Plant a "garden of goodness" in your life today: First, plant peas: patience; peace; and prayer. Next, plant squash: squash gossip; squash anger; and squash meanness. Then plant lettuce: lettuce love the Lord; lettuce be gentle; lettuce be joyful; lettuce be self-controlled. Finish with turnips: turnip when needed; turnip with joy; turnip with helping hands; turnip with determination.

**Table Talk:**
- What other "vegetables" can you plant in your life?
- What other "peas" can you come up with? Squash? Lettuce? Turnips?
- How do these things "feed" others?

**Vitamins and Minerals:** "By their fruit you will recognize them" (Matthew 7:20).

---

[21] Mary Beth Lagerborg and Karen J. Parks, *Beyond Macaroni & Cheese* (Grand Rapids: Zondervan, 1998), 39.
[22] Food Trivia Page: http://www3.nd.edu/~cjohnsol/foodtriv.htm

# Watch Them Jiggle

**Mealtime Prayer:** God wants our faith to be strong and unmovable like Him. Look around and find something solid, such as the table or the walls. (Hopefully not your food!) As you pray for your meal, ask God to make your faith solid like that item.

**Appetizer:** Did you know that you can grow seeds in Jell-O® and observe their root structures? Did you know that a teaspoon of Jell-O dissolved in a cup of warm water makes hair gel? (Please get parental permission before attempting this!) What is your favorite flavor of Jell-O? Why?

**Main Course:** Have you ever heard someone say, "I'm so lucky"? Where do all good things ultimately come from? From luck? How can people without God be like jiggly Jell-O? How does lack of belief affect a person's emotions? Their lives? Remember, Jell-O may be great for dessert, but we have Someone much solider to put our faith in!

**Table Talk:**
- How does knowing that God is always the same, always "solid" help you to stand firm (for example, He is always true, so I'll tell the truth)?
- What can we tell others about God's solidness (for example, God always hears our prayers)?
- How does having solid belief in God affect you?

**Vitamins and Minerals:** "Every good and perfect gift is from above, coming down from the Father of the heavenly lights, who does not change like shifting shadows" (James 1:17).

# Better Than Spinach!

**Mealtime Prayer:** "Lord, when I am weak, You are strong. Help me to get more out of Your Word than in any physical food. Amen."

**Appetizer:** Care to test your strength? Have a thumb-war contest. Intertwine your fingers with another family member's, thumbs sticking up. The goal is to "pin" your partner's thumb with your own. Start by saying, "One, two, three, four, I declare a thumb war. Begin!"

**Main Course:** Did you know that eating tons of spinach will not make you big and strong? (Sorry, Popeye!) Spinach does not make your muscles bigger, but it does provide you with iron, calcium, vitamin B, and folic acid. Any idea how these help your body?

What (actually Who) can make you truly strong? How does God's love make you confident? His presence? His faithfulness?

To help you remember God's strength, write the following powerful promises on a piece of paper and "digest" (think about) one daily: Psalm 89:21, 2; 119:28; Ephesians 3:16; 2 Thessalonians 2:16–17; 3:3. Watch your spiritual muscles grow!

**Table Talk:**
- What other powerful promises do you know from God's Word (Proverbs and Psalms have lots)?
- How will these verses strengthen your spiritual muscles?
- Along with reading God's Word, what are other ways to strengthen your spiritual muscles?

**Vitamins and Minerals:** "Strengthen me according to your word" (Psalm 119:28).

# Eating It Up

**Mealtime Prayer:** Thank God for the many meals around the world.

**Appetizer:** Did you know that the Jews in Jesus' day obeyed strict laws, which told them what to eat and how to dress? But Jesus didn't look at the outside; He looked at the heart. Peter was willing to break the laws of the Jews to share Jesus. When would you have to break a law to share Jesus?

**Main Course:** Peter was one of Jesus' disciples. As a Jew, Peter couldn't eat certain animals, such as pigs . . . until he had a vision. Read Acts 10:11–15. What did this vision tell Peter? Later, Peter realized that God was talking about different people as well as different food. Before Jesus came to earth, God mainly worked through His chosen people, the Jews. After the vision, Peter knew that God wanted all people to receive the good news that Jesus' death was for everyone! Why was this so important?

**Table Talk:**
- Why does God care about all people, not just those of a certain faith?
- What "laws" (such as, don't eat with the unpopular kid) might need to be broken? Why?
- Name three people in your neighborhood or school whom God loves just as much as He loves you. How can you share Jesus with them?

**Vitamins and Minerals:** "God does not show favoritism but accepts men from every nation" (Acts 10:34–35).

# What's for Dinner?

**Mealtime Prayer:** (Tune: "Hi Ho, Hi Ho")
"We know, we know, from whom all good things flow. We thank Him then, we say Amen, We know, we know, we know, we know!"

**Appetizer:** If you lived in a different country and asked, "What's for dinner?" you might hear: "Lasagna" (Italy); "Goulash" (Hungary); "Pork and Sauerkraut" (Germany); "Borscht," or Cabbage soup (Russia).

Can you think of others?

**Main Course:** Would you be surprised if you asked, "What's for dinner?" and were answered, "Rocks, sticks, and grass"? Why? Why do your parents give you the best they can? Why does God give you the best?

Jesus said, "Which of you, if his son asks for bread, will give him a stone? . . . If you, then, though you are evil, know how to give good gifts to your children, how much more will your Father in heaven give good gifts to those who ask him!" (Matthew 7:9, 11). What do you have to do to get these good gifts from God?

**Table Talk:**
- Since your parents love you, will they give you anything you ask for? Why or why not? Will God?
- What should we ask for? Why?
- Name five good things God's given you.

**Vitamins and Minerals:** "Everyone who asks receives; he who seeks finds; and to him who knocks, the door will be opened" (Matthew 7:8).

**GOD/GOD'S PROVISION**

# Surprise Inspection

**Mealtime Prayer:**
"For this our daily food,
For our health and happiness,
For our salvation and our future heavenly home,
Give us a thankful heart, O Lord. Amen."

**Appetizer:** Surprise inspection! If your parents took a surprise inspection of your room, what would they discover? How would you feel? What would you find if you inspected your parents' room?

**Main Course:** How would you feel if this were the day you stood before Jesus? Your parents may inspect your room and closets, but what will Jesus "inspect"? Will He be pleased by what He sees? Why or why not?

If Jesus will say, "Well done, good and faithful servant!" (Matthew 25:21) to those who faithfully build a relationship with Him, what would you be willing to do to get this response?

**Table Talk:**
- If you had to stand before Christ today, what might He say?
- What can you do to make sure that your life pleases God?
- What will be the coolest things about seeing Jesus?

**Vitamins and Minerals:** "We must all appear before the judgment seat of Christ, that each one may receive what is due him for the things done while in the body, whether good or bad" (2 Corinthians 5:10).

# Holidays and Special Occasions

# Birthday: It's Original

**Mealtime Prayer:** Have each family member thank God for the birthday person when you pray.

**Appetizer:** Bible Birthday Trivia:
  Q: How many birthdays did Methuselah have? (*Answer: 969*)
  Q: How old was Abraham when Isaac was born? (*Answer: 100*)
  Q: How old was Jesus when He first taught in the temple? (*Answer: 12*)
  Q: How many earthly years did Jesus live? (*Answer: 33*)
  Q: How old are you?

**Main Course:** When an artist paints a special painting and decides not to make another one like it, it is called an original. Why is an original so valuable?

You, the birthday person, are special and valuable because you are an original. There is no one else like you in the whole world. For every year you are celebrating, your family members will give reasons why you are special. If you are eight years old, they must think of eight reasons. And by the way—happy birthday!

**Table Talk:**
  • Why did God make only one of you?
  • How are you different from the other people in your family?
  • How can God use you in a special way?

**Vitamins and Minerals:** "I praise you because I am fearfully and wonderfully made; your works are wonderful, I know that full well" (Psalm 139:14).

# New Year's Day:
# If at First You Don't Succeed

**Mealtime Prayer:** Thank God for His love and care. Ask Him to show you His will for the coming year.

**Appetizer:** Have each person share something he or she wants to do this year.

**Main Course:** Happy New Year! At the beginning of each new year, people often make plans. Why do you think they do that?

Did you know that God planned your whole life before you were born? Psalm 139:16 says, "All the days ordained for me were written in your book before one of them came to be." Why do you think God did that?

Proverbs 16:3 says, "Commit to the LORD whatever you do, and your plans will succeed." What does it mean to succeed? How can we be successful in life?

**Table Talk:**
- How can we know God's plans for our lives?
- Why are God's plans best?
- What do you think God has planned for you this year?

**Vitamins and Minerals:** "'For I know the plans I have for you,' declares the LORD, 'plans to prosper you and not to harm you, plans to give you hope and a future'" (Jeremiah 29:11).

# Valentine's Day: Show-and-tell

**Mealtime Prayer:** Thank God for the many ways He shows His love to you. Give examples. Thank Him for the people who love you and for those you love.

**Appetizer:** Have each person tell the other family members one thing he or she loves about each of them.

**Main Course:** Valentine's Day is a special day to let others know we love them. What did you do today to show your love for someone? What tells you you're loved? What are other ways that we can show our love for one another? (For example, play practical jokes, give breakfast in bed, clean the kitchen.)

**Table Talk:**
- How does God show that He loves us?
- Why do you think God wants us to love one another?
- How can children show love to their parents? How can parents show love to their children?
- How can we show our love for God?

**Vitamins and Minerals:** "Dear friends, let us love one another, for love comes from God. Everyone who loves has been born of God and knows God" (1 John 4:7).

# April Fool's Day: Who's a Fool?

**Mealtime Prayer:** As you ask God to bless your food, thank Him for times of fun and laughter.

**Appetizer:** Hey! Did you know that tonight you get to stay up all night? You may have dessert before you eat your dinner, and you don't have to help with dishes or do chores—*April Fool's!*

**Main Course:** What April Fool's tricks did you play today? What tricks were played on you? What was the best April Fool's trick you've ever played on someone else?

April Fool's Day is a day when we can play fun tricks on our friends and family. Why do you think it's called April Fool's Day? What is a fool?

Psalm 14:1 says, "The fool says in his heart, 'There is no God.'" Why is someone who doesn't believe in God a fool? What are some other things that fools don't believe in?

**Table Talk:**
- How can you keep from being a fool?
- Who do you think is happier, a wise person or a foolish person? Why?
- How do you think God feels about fun? Why?

**Vitamins and Minerals:** "Our mouths were filled with laughter, our tongues with songs of joy" (Psalm 126:2).

# Good Friday: Who Took the Sun?

**Mealtime Prayer:** After you give thanks for your food, have each person thank Jesus in their own words for dying on the cross for them.

**Appetizer:** Over seven hundred years before Jesus was born, the prophet Isaiah predicted that He would be crucified (Isaiah 53:5). How did he know this would happen? What else was predicted about Jesus?

What can you predict about next week? How accurate would you be?

**Main Course:** The more specific a prediction is, the less likely it will come true. Read the story of the crucifixion of Jesus in Luke 23:33–47 and then read Isaiah 53:3–9. How accurate was Isaiah? Why do you think God told Isaiah and other prophets what would happen to Jesus?

**Table Talk:**
- Why do you think the sun went dark?
- What would you have thought if you had been one of the soldiers?
- How is Jesus like the sun?
- If God loves Jesus, why didn't He do something to help Him?

**Vitamins and Minerals:** "God demonstrated his own love for us in this: While we were still sinners, Christ died for us" (Romans 5:8).

# Easter Sunday: Sunday Surprise

**Mealtime Prayer:** Thank Jesus that because of His death and resurrection we can have the hope of living forever.

**Appetizer:** What are the most important events of the past ten years? Of all history?

**Main Course:** Two days after Jesus died, Mary Magdalene and Mary the mother of James went to Jesus' tomb. How do you think they felt when they saw an angel there instead of Jesus' body? (Read Matthew 28:5–7.)

The soldiers who were guarding the tomb were paid a lot of money to say that Jesus' disciples stole His body (Matthew 28:12–13). What really happened to Jesus' body? Why do you think the soldiers were paid to lie? If you had been one of the soldiers, what would you have thought and done?

After Jesus' resurrection (rising from the dead), He appeared to some of His friends and disciples. What would you have said to Jesus if you had been there?

**Table Talk:**
- Why is Jesus' resurrection the most important event in all of history? How is it more important than the events you mentioned earlier?
- What does Jesus' resurrection mean to you?
- Why should we tell others about Jesus' resurrection?

**Vitamins and Minerals:** "Christ died and returned to life so that he might be the Lord of both the dead and the living" (Romans 14:9).

# Mother's Day: Marvelous Moms

**Mealtime Prayer:** Have each person tell Mom why she is marvelous. Follow this activity by thanking God for her.

**Appetizer:** Marvelous Moms' Bible Quiz:

Q: Who prayed for a son and named him Samuel? (*Answer: Hannah.*)

Q: Who gave birth to a son at a very old age? (*Answer: Sarah.*)

Q: Who was the mother of Joseph, Jacob's son? (*Answer: Rachel.*)

Q: Who was the mother of John the Baptist? (*Answer: Elizabeth.*)

Q: Who was the mother of Jesus? (*Answer: Mary.*)

Q: What did the mother skunk say to her children before dinner? (*Answer: Let's spray.*)

**Main Course:** Why are mothers important to a family? Name all the things your mother does for you from the time you get up in the morning until the time you go to bed at night. What are ways you can show your appreciation for everything she does?

**Table Talk:**

- Why do you think God created mothers?
- Why did Jesus need a mother?
- Tell your mom you love her and why.

**Vitamins and Minerals:** "Charm is deceptive, and beauty is fleeting; but a woman who fears the LORD is to be praised" (Proverbs 31:30).

# Memorial Day: Flowers and Flags

**Mealtime Prayer:** Thank God for your country, your freedom, and His love.

**Appetizer:** The first Memorial Day in the United States was May 30, 1868. General John Alexander Logan ordered that the graves of those who had died in the American Civil War be decorated. Why do you think he did that?

**Main Course:** Do you know people who have served their country by being in the Army, Navy, Air Force, or Marines? People who are in the armed forces make many sacrifices to protect their country and keep it safe. What are some you can think of? They may even have to fight in a war and be willing to die while fighting for their country and for freedom.

Memorial Day is a special holiday to honor men and women who have died during wartime. Families and friends put flowers or flags on the graves. Many cities have parades, and some families celebrate with friends and relatives. How do you celebrate Memorial Day?

**Table Talk:**
- The Bible tells us of someone who was willing to die so we could have freedom from sin. Who was that person?
- How can we celebrate our freedom from sin?
- What would you be willing to die for?

**Vitamins and Minerals:** "Greater love has no one than this, that he lay down his life for his friends" (John 15:13).

# Father's Day: Fabulous Fathers

**Mealtime Prayer:** Have each person tell Dad why he is fabulous. Thank God for your father while you pray.

**Appetizer:** Fabulous Father Bible Quiz:
    Q: Who became a father when he was one hundred years old? (*Answer: Abraham.*)
    Q: Who gave his son a colorful coat? (*Answer: Jacob.*)
    Q: Who was King Solomon's father? (*Answer: David.*)
    Q: Who was the father of John the Baptist? (*Answer: Zechariah.*)
    Q: What did the colt say to his mother? (*Answer: Where's my fodder?*)

**Main Course:** Why are fathers important to a family? What does your father do for you each day to show that he loves you? How can you show your father that you love him and appreciate all that he does for you? Proverbs 23:22 says, "Listen to your father, who gave you life." What does that mean?

**Table Talk:**
- How can you bring joy to your father?
- Why is it wise to listen to your father?
- Why did God create fathers?
- Tell your father you love him and why.

**Vitamins and Minerals:** "Children's children are a crown to the aged, and parents are the pride of their children" (Proverbs 17:6).

# Independence Day: Let's Party!

**Mealtime Prayer:** Thank God for the freedom to worship, and ask Him to bless our country.

**Appetizer:** What did one firecracker say to the other firecracker? (*Answer: "My pop's bigger than your pop!"*)

**Main Course:** How do you celebrate your country's independence? Why? When the people from England settled in America, they formed individual colonies. Eventually there were 13 colonies along the eastern coast. On July 4, 1776, the leaders of the colonies adopted the Declaration of Independence, which gave them freedom from the British government. This meant they could make their own decisions and worship God the way they wanted. The people were so happy they celebrated with marching bands and the chiming of city bells. Since then, July 4 has been celebrated in the United States as Independence Day. Today, people in the U.S. celebrate with parades, family picnics, and fireworks.

**Table Talk:**
- What's your favorite part of the celebration? Why?
- Why is religious freedom so important?
- If you were one of the colonial leaders, what would you have included in the Declaration of Independence?

**Vitamins and Minerals:** "Blessed is the nation whose God is the LORD" (Psalm 33:12).

# Thanksgiving Day: Gobble, Gobble

**Mealtime Prayer:** Hold hands while you pray. Have each person tell God something he or she is grateful for.

**Appetizer:** Preserve holiday memories with a Thanksgiving Day journal. Every year record the events of the day, the people with whom you celebrated, and specific blessings you are thankful for. What would you include this year?

**Main Course:** If you could invent a holiday to celebrate, what would it be? Why?

In 1620 Pilgrims from England came to America for religious freedom. They faced many hardships and many died. The American Indians helped the Pilgrims by teaching them how to farm and fish. After the first harvest, the Pilgrims and Indians celebrated with a huge feast—turkey, corn, and pumpkin pie! They thanked God for His goodness throughout the year.

In 1863 President Abraham Lincoln appointed a special day of thanksgiving.
In Canada Thanksgiving is celebrated in October rather than November. If you don't have a thanksgiving day in your country, choose a day to have your own celebration.

**Table Talk:**
- If you had been a Pilgrim, what would you have been thankful for?
- What do we have today that the Pilgrims did not have?
- What do you think you'll be thankful for next year?

**Vitamins and Minerals:** "Give thanks to the LORD, for he is good. *His love endures forever*" (Psalm 136:1, italics added).

# Christmas Eve: No Vacancy

**Mealtime Prayer:** Thank God that He keeps all of His promises.

**Appetizer:** Where is the most unusual place you have ever spent the night?

**Main Course:** The prophet Isaiah wrote that Jesus would be born to a virgin (see Vitamins and Minerals). Micah said He would be born in Bethlehem (Micah 5:2).

Seven hundred years later, an angel told the virgin Mary she would have a baby who would be the Son of God (Luke 1:26–33). Caesar Augustus decided to count all the people under Roman rule. So Mary and her fiancé, Joseph, went to Bethlehem to be counted. When they arrived, the inn was full, so they stayed in a stable where they could rest and keep warm (Luke 2:1–7). How could Micah have known about the Roman count? Try predicting something for the next year. (Write it down and check it next year.)

**Table Talk:**
- What does the fulfillment of these prophecies tell you about the Bible?
- If the innkeeper knew Mary was going to be the mother of God's Son, do you think he would have acted differently? Why?
- What's your favorite part of Christmas Eve? What could you do to understand what it was like for Mary and Joseph?

**Vitamins and Minerals:** "The LORD himself will give you a sign: The virgin will be with child and will give birth to a son, and will call him Immanuel" (Isaiah 7:14).

# Christmas Day: It's a Boy!

**_Mealtime Prayer:_** What gifts has God given you? Thank Him for these gifts and the gift of His Son.

**_Appetizer:_** Give a verbal gift to each person at the table by giving him or her a specific compliment.

**_Main Course:_** Imagine being in the stable (probably a cave) with Mary. What would it have been like? What would it have smelled like?

Something exciting happened while Joseph and Mary were resting in the stable in Bethlehem. Read about it in Luke 2:6–11.

**_Table Talk:_**
- If you were one of the shepherds, how would you have felt? What would you have done?
- Where can we find Jesus today?
- What gifts can we give Him?
- What should we do with the news of His birth?

**_Vitamins and Minerals:_** "The Word became flesh and made his dwelling among us" (John 1:14).

# Boxing Day: What's in the Box?

**Mealtime Prayer:** As you thank God for His blessings, thank Him for opportunities to give gifts to others.

**Appetizer:** Give everyone an empty box. Have them put small gifts in their box and bring it back to the table. Exchange boxes.

**Main Course:** Have you ever heard of Boxing Day? It's not a day when two people get into a boxing ring and punch each other. Boxing Day refers to gift boxes, and if you live in England, Wales, or parts of Canada, you know what it is.

Today, in Canada, Boxing Day is the biggest shopping day of the year. Store owners slash prices and eager shoppers search for bargains or begin Christmas shopping for the next year. If people get too greedy, however, it may turn into a real "boxing day" after all!

In days of old, landowners or wealthy people gave gifts of money to servants, tradespeople, and other common people. The gifts became known as Christmas boxes and were given on December 26, the day after Christmas. What would you put in imaginary boxes for a cook, laundry person, housecleaner, and carpenter?

**Table Talk:**
- How do you think the people felt when they received their gift boxes?
- What do you think they did with their gifts of money?
- Who could you give gifts to after Christmas?

**Vitamins and Minerals:** "It is more blessed to give than to receive" (Acts 20:35).

# New Years Eve: Looking Back

**Mealtime Prayer:** Have someone read the following prayer:
"Thank You for blessings You give us each day,
For times to work and times to play.
Thank You for blessings of health and cheer,
And all of our blessings throughout the year. Amen."

**Appetizer:** Get out pen and paper for each person. Have everyone make a list of God's blessings, or good gifts, this past year. The first one to get to 10 blessings wins. (Give candy as prizes.)

**Main Course:** New Year's Eve is the end of another year. Many families celebrate with parties and stay up until midnight. What do you do on New Year's Eve? Why do you think people celebrate it? What is so important about it?

New Year's Eve is also a time to look back over the past year and thank God for His blessings. Proverbs 3:33 says, "[God] blesses the home of the righteous." Proverbs 28:20 says, "A faithful man will be richly blessed." What do you think these verses mean?

**Table Talk:**
- How do we receive God's blessings?
- Sometimes blessings don't seem like them at the time. What difficult things this year can you now see were blessings in disguise?
- What is the best thing that happened to you this past year?

**Vitamins and Minerals:** "O LORD Almighty, blessed is the man who trusts in you" (Psalm 84:12).

**GOD'S CARE/GOD'S PROVISION/THANKFULNESS**

# Anniversary: You First

**Mealtime Prayer:** Tell your spouse what you appreciate about him or her. Have the children say what they like about your marriage. Thank God for each other.

**Appetizer:** Bible Couples Trivia Game:

    Q: Who was married to Abraham? (*Answer: Sarah.*)
    Q: Who was the husband of Pricilla? (*Answer: Aquila.*)
    Q: What was the name of Isaac's wife? (*Answer: Rebekah.*)
    Q: Who was Ruth's second husband? (*Answer: Boaz.*)
    Q: Who was married to Zechariah? (*Answer: Elizabeth.*)
    Q: What was the name of Hosea's wife? (*Answer: Gomer.*)
    Q: Who was Jezebel's husband? (*Answer: Ahab.*)

**Main Course:** Read the definition of love from 1 Corinthians 13:4–7. Why do you think love is defined by actions rather than feelings?

**Table Talk:**

- Think of specific ways you see love in your parents' marriage. What are they?
- How does a good marriage help the entire family?
- How can your parents continue to show love to each other? How can you show love to them?

**Vitamins and Minerals for Husbands:** "Husbands, love your wives, just as Christ loved the church and gave himself up for her" (Ephesians 5:25).

**Vitamins and Minerals for Wives:** "Wives, submit to your husbands, as is fitting in the Lord" (Colossians 3:18).

# Theme Meals

# Search for Treasure

**Mealtime Prayer:** "Lord, thank You for the treasures seated around this table. Amen."

**Appetizer:** Blackbeard was one of the most famous pirates of all time. If you could give yourself a pirate name, what would it be? The name of Blackbeard's ship was *Queen Anne's Revenge*. If you had a ship, what would you call her? Why?

**Pirate Night:** Prepare a treasure hunt. Hide a stockpile of "treasure" in your house—things like a Bible, a picture of your family, and memory verse cards. (What other "treasures" can you hide?)

Make a map that will lead to these treasures. Fix a hearty pirate meal, such as stew or meat and potatoes. Dress your family up in scarves, eye patches, and fake moustaches. (Washable mascara works great.) After the hunt, have your meal—then read Matthew:19–20.

**Table Talk:**
- What type of treasures do moth and rust destroy?
- What type of treasure do you store up in heaven? How?
- What things that we found during the treasure hunt will last for eternity? What makes the difference?

**Vitamins and Minerals:** "Where your treasure is, there your heart will be also" (Matthew 6:21).

# Upside—down Gospel

**Mealtime Prayer:** "Lord, help me to follow Your ways, even if they are different from the ones I desire. Amen."

**Appetizer:** Tonight, do everything backward. Start with dessert, then eat your meal! (Try a few things upside-down, such as using your spoon bottom side up!) Say your prayer at the end of the meal.

**Backward Night:** Christianity is often thought of as a backward and upside-down religion. Read Luke 6:27–30. Now play a backward/upside-down version of "Red Light, Green Light." For this game, the red represents the Lord's blood, and you proceed. On green, you stop. Take turns being the caller.

**Table Talk:**
- If someone is mean to you, the world says, "Show who's boss." What does Jesus say? (See v. 27.) How will this affect the mean person?
- If someone hits you or takes your things, the world says, "Fight back." What does Jesus say? (See v. 29.) What difference will this response make?
- The world says, "Protect your stuff—you deserve what you have." What does Jesus say? (See v. 30.) Why can you do this without worry?
- Can you think of any other backward, upside-down examples? How do they work?

**Vitamins and Minerals:** "Love your enemies, do good to them, and lend to them without expecting to get anything back. Then your reward will be great, and you will be sons of the Most High, because he is kind to the ungrateful and wicked" (Luke 6:35).

# Getting to Know You

**Mealtime Prayer:** Thank the Lord for your favorite food on the table. Then ask God to show you what's important to Him.

**Appetizer:** How well do you know your parents? What are their ages? Their eye colors? (Without looking!) Their favorite hobbies?

**Family Discovery Night:** Cook a family favorite today. Do you know your family well? As you spend time with each other, you discover likes and dislikes. Give each family member a list of these questions. Try to guess their response before they answer. Name your . . .

| | | |
|---|---|---|
| Coolest experience: | Bravest thing done: | Favorite holiday: |
| Favorite summer activity: | Special skill or talent: | Favorite food: |
| Least favorite food: | Favorite Bible story: | Favorite cartoon: |
| Favorite animal: | Favorite place to talk to God: | Favorite pastime: |
| Favorite month: | Favorite thing to wear: | Favorite verse: |

**Table Talk:**
- How does listening to each other prove you care?
- How can you get to know Jesus better?
- What one action today showed your love to a family member? What showed your love to Jesus?
- What did you learn about Jesus recently that you didn't know before?

**Vitamins and Minerals:** "Whoever has my commands and obeys them, he is the one who loves me. He who loves me will be loved by my Father, and I too will love him and show myself to him" (John 14:21).

**GAMES/LISTENING/LOVE**

# Put a Little Sugar in That Hospitali-tea!

**Mealtime Prayer:** "Lord, thank you that I have friends and family, and that You take such good care of me! Amen."

**Appetizer:** Did you know that tea is a natural source of fluoride, which helps to prevent tooth decay—unless, of course, you add sugar to that tea!

What starts with "t," ends with "t," and is filled with "t"? (*Answer: A teapot.*)

**Company's Coming:** Company's coming for dinner! It is your family's time to shine. How does hospitality (a warm welcome) make others feel special? Why does it make God proud? When your company arrives, here are three ways to make them feel welcome:

1. Greet your guests at the door and welcome them into your home.
2. Provide refreshments. (Make your guest a cup of tea!)
3. Sit and visit with your guests. Find a conversation topic that you both enjoy. Ask questions about them and what they like to do.

**Table Talk:**

- How many other ways can you think of to show hospitality?
- When was a time you felt welcomed into someone else's home? What did they do to make you feel that way? What can you learn from their good example?

**Vitamins and Minerals:** "Share with God's people who are in need. Practice hospitality" (Romans 12:13).

# Aloha!

**Mealtime Prayer:** *He aloha lani ke kau nei, Ma ko Iesû lâ lae, Ma kona po'o he lei ali'i, He leo ho'omaika'i.* "Majestic sweetness sits enthroned, On my Redeemer's brow, His head with radiant glories crowned, His lips with grace overflow."[23]

**Appetizer:** Did you know that in the nineteenth century over nine hundred Christian hymns were translated into Hawaiian? (Today's prayer is one of them.) They are still sung today. Favorite foods of a luau are laulau (pork cooked in leaves), fish, and ahupia (coconut milk custard).

**Hawaiian Luau:** Before your meal, string popcorn and tie the strings into necklaces for mock leis. Prepare fish for dinner. After your meal, do the limbo under a broomstick.

Aloha! Hawaiian leis are given to show appreciation and friendship. Today, it's popular for leis to be made of flowers, leaves, and vines. How would it feel to wear a lei like that? What would it smell like? The Bible speaks of garlands of beauty. Read Proverbs 1:8–9. Why is obedience beautiful?

**Table Talk:**
- What have you done today that "adorns your neck with beauty"?
- If you had a chance to visit Hawaii for the first time, what new thing would you try?
- Why do you think translating hymns into Hawaiian was important to the first missionaries? What's your favorite song to sing to God?

**Vitamins and Minerals:** "[Wisdom] will set a garland of grace on your head" (Proverbs 4:9).

[23] Hawaii Luau Online: http://www.si.edu/folklife/vfest/hawaii/himeni.htm

# Fortune Promises

**Mealtime Prayer:** "Lord, may Your promises strengthen my soul just as food strengthens my body. Amen."

**Appetizer:** Did you know that you can order cookies with scriptures inside?[24] Did you know that chopsticks have been traced back as far as the third century B.C.? Today, chopsticks are used in Japan, Korea, Vietnam, and China, making them the world's second most popular tool for eating. The most popular? Fingers![25]

**Chinese Food:** Make or pick up Chinese food. Don't forget the chopsticks! Make a pot of green tea to go with your meal. Use candles for lighting.

Look up these Bible promises (Joshua 1:5; Psalm 32:8; Matthew 10:32; 28:20; John 14:3, 13, 23; 15:4; Acts 2:17). Write them on slips of paper and place one promise under every plate. During the meal, have each person look under his or her plate and read the promise. Discuss what they mean.

**Table Talk:**
- Fortunes are humorous guesses about what might happen in the future, but they rarely come true. Why?
- Bible promises are fact. How do we know that what God says will come true?

**Vitamins and Minerals:** "You know with all your heart and soul that not one of all the good promises the LORD your God gave you has failed" (Joshua 23:14).

---

[24] Evangelistic Foods, P.O. Box 16410, Minneapolis, MN 55416, 1-800-743-0142
[25] Oriental Food Web site: http://www.orientalfood.com

**GOD'S WORD/PROMISES/TRUTH**

# Bible Riddles

**Mealtime Prayer:** Pray the shortest prayer in the Bible: "Lord, help me!" (Matthew 15:25).

**Appetizer:** After dinner, play Bible Trivia with your family, teaming younger children with a parent. Rules:

1. Take turns making up and asking trivia questions. (You must know the answer!)
2. Start with easy ones.

Don't keep points or compare yourselves with others. Instead, enjoy how much you've learned about God's Word!

**Bible Trivia Night:** Fix a meal of biblical foods, such as bread and fish (Matthew 15:36), honey (Mark 1:6), figs (James 3:12), grapes, and milk (1 Corinthians 9:7).

Before you eat, ask the Bible riddle found in Judges 14:14. Don't give away the answer before it's time! Do you know the answer? (Honey from a lion!—see Judges 14:9.)

**Table Talk:**

- Why is it important to know God's Word?
- What's different from the way you live today and the way the people of the Bible lived? What's the same?
- Do you know any riddles? Share them with your family.

**Vitamins and Minerals:** "Each one should test his own actions. Then he can take pride in himself, without comparing himself to somebody else" (Galatians 6:4).

# Fun with Fondue

**Mealtime Prayer:** "Thank You, Lord, for Your bountiful blessings. May my every action, great or small, be acceptable to You this night. Amen."

**Appetizer:** Did you know that Jesus was baptized in the Jordan River? That is the same river that God told Naaman to dip in! What else happened in the Jordan River?

**Fondue Night:** Serve fondue tonight. If you don't want to serve a whole fondue meal, try a dessert fondue—dip fresh fruit and chunks of pound cake into melted chocolate!
Before you begin the meal, read 2 Kings 5:10–14. Naaman thought dipping in the water was too simple, but what did God want Naaman to discover? What's more important, obeying God in big things or obeying Him in small things? Why?

Each time you dip your fondue tonight, mention one simple thing you can do for God, such as holding the door open at the store or waving to a neighbor. How many different ideas did you come up with?

**Table Talk:**
- Were there magical powers in the river that healed Naaman? How do you know?
- Who healed Naaman? Why?
- What did Naaman prove by following God's commands?

**Vitamins and Minerals:** "[Naaman] said, 'Now I know that there is no God in all the world except in Israel'" (2 Kings 5:15).

# Home on the Range

**Mealtime Prayer:** "It's been a long day, We're dusty and tired. This grub smells better than most! We bow down our heads, Give thanks for this food, For in nature, God is our host."

**Camping Trip:** Plan a camping trip, or set up a tent in your backyard. Take a deep breath. What do you smell? What do you hear? Build a campfire. Cook hot dogs, beans, and s'mores. When you're finished eating, go on a nature hike. (Watch where you're stepping! Keep your eyes open for scat, or animal droppings.) Use these questions as a guide:

Q: How many different-shaped leaves can you find? Which is your favorite? Why?

Q: What clues prove that animals have visited this place?

Q: Examine a flower. What details amaze you?

**Table Talk:** When you come back around the campfire, answer:

- How are God's qualities clearly seen in what He has made?
- What did you learn about God tonight? (Examples: He pays attention to detail. He loves color and texture.)
- How can you thank God for what He has made?

**Vitamins and Minerals:** "Since the creation of the world God's invisible qualities—his eternal power and divine nature—have been clearly seen, being understood from what has been made, so that men are without excuse" (Romans 1:20).

# Hooray for Grandparents!

**Mealtime Prayer:** "Thank You, Lord, that You never change. You loved us yesterday. You love us today. And You'll love us for every tomorrow. Amen."

**Appetizer:** Did you know that Big Macs were invented in 1968? How old were your grandparents then? Can your grandparents name the ingredients of a Big Mac? (Two all-beef patties, special sauce, lettuce, cheese, pickles, onions, on a sesame seed bun!)

**Grandparent Night:** Invite your grandparents over for dinner. (If you don't have grandparents nearby, adopt some!) Fix their favorite food as a surprise.

No matter how things change over the years, who never changes? How is God's care of you now the same as it will be when you're older? Read Isaiah 46:4.

**Table Talk:** Ask the grandparents these questions:
- What was your favorite meal as a child? What's your favorite meal now?
- How did your parents cook their food? What new appliances do you use today?
- What is one way God has taken care of you over the years? How does God take care of you now?

*For the kids:*
- What types of food do you think you'll eat when you are your grandparents' age?
- What types of appliances do you think you'll use?

**Vitamins and Minerals:** "Gray hair is a crown of splendor; it is attained by a righteous life" (Proverbs 16:31).

# Let's Bake!

**Mealtime Prayer:** Pray: "O Lord God almighty, who is like You? And who is like me, Your creation?" Then thank God for things about you that you like.

**Appetizer:** Make a recipe card for yourself. What things did God mix together to make you? What part of you is the icing?

**Bake Together:** Plan to bake a treat together, such as cookies or a cake, after your meal. It doesn't have to be from scratch; a boxed mix will work well. Work as a team.

Just as you knew what you were going to bake, God knew you from the beginning. Read Psalm 139:16. Who knows the number of your days? Read Colossians 1:16. Who were you created for? How do you bring God pleasure? Why does He simply love you for you?

**Table Talk:**
- How does baking something special make you feel?
- How do you think God felt when He created you?
- What can you do to make your special treat even more unique? Try it!

**Vitamins and Minerals:** "You created my inmost being; you knit me together in my mother's womb. I praise you because I am fearfully and wonderfully made; your works are wonderful, I know that full well" (Psalm 139:13–14).

# Jesus and I Make a Great "Pear"

**Mealtime Prayer:** (Tune: "Yankee Doodle")
"We thank You, Lord, for daily bread, for rain and sunny weather.
We thank You, Lord, for this our food, and that we are together."

**Appetizer:** How do you and your best friend make a great "pear" (pair)?

**Friend for Dinner:** Invite a friend for dinner. Serve things that "go together," such as peanut butter and jelly, macaroni and cheese, or corn bread and chili. Fix bananas and pears for dessert.

The best way to ripen pears is to seal them in a plastic bag with a couple of ripe bananas, leaving them at room temperature. The bananas help the pears ripen quickly and evenly. Like pears, we need buddies. Why are buddies important? Who is the only perfect Friend? Read these verses that tell why Jesus is such a good friend.

- First Peter 1:16. What type of example is Jesus?
- Hebrews 13:5. Will Jesus ever move away?
- Philippians 4:13. How can Jesus help you?

**Table Talk:**
- What makes a good friend? What are three reasons that Jesus is the best Friend of all?
- How does your friend help you become a better person? How will Jesus help you become the person God designed you to be?

**Vitamins and Minerals:** "There is a friend who sticks closer than a brother" (Proverbs 18:24).

COMPANIONSHIP/FRIENDS/RIGHTEOUSNESS

# Pizza Party!

**Mealtime Prayer:** "Lord, thank You for the variety of foods You have blessed me with. Thank You also for the different parts of my life. May my body, mind, and soul belong to You today. Amen."

**Appetizer:** Did you know that 350 million tons of frozen pizza are sold every year? At home in North America, the average family eats pizza 30 times a year![26] How many does your family eat in one month?

**Pizza Night:** Order or make everyone's favorite—pizza! Decorate your house like an old-fashioned pizza parlor. Play '50s music.

Just like a pizza, how is your life split into different sections? What are those different sections (home, school, friends, recreation, church, sports, etc.)? God wants to be involved in every part. Why? Think of one way that God can help in each part of your life.

**Table Talk:**
- If your life were a pizza with 10 slices, how many slices would you say belong to God?
- Which slices of your life are hardest to let Him control?
- Which slices do you enjoy the most?

**Vitamins and Minerals:** "Love the Lord your God with all your heart and with all your soul and with all your strength and with all your mind" (Luke 10:27).

[26] Pizza Pieer home page: http://www.pizzapieer.com/

# Rainbow Salad!

**Mealtime Prayer:** "Be present at our table, Lord. Be here and everywhere adored. These mercies bless, and grant that we may feast in Paradise with thee."
—*John Cennick, 1741*

**Appetizer:** Did you know that there's a rainbow in heaven? Revelation 4:3 says a rainbow, which looks like an emerald, circles God's throne!

**Picnic:** Plan an outdoor picnic for your family. If it's colder weather, lay out a picnic blanket in your living room. Prepare fruit for a Rainbow Salad. Before the meal, have family members take turns mixing one of each color:

- Red: strawberries, watermelon, or cherries
- Orange: orange slices or cantaloupe
- Yellow: bananas or peaches
- Green: apples or honeydew melon
- Blue: blueberries
- Purple: grapes or blackberries

Add whipped cream to your salad and enjoy!

The rainbow is a promise from God. Read Genesis 9:9–11. What was God's promise? Who did God give the promise to? How does this promise affect us today?

**Table Talk:**
- God always keeps His promises. What are some of these promises?
- How does knowing God's promises are reliable help you?
- What is your favorite color of the rainbow? Why?

**Vitamins and Minerals:** "I have set my rainbow in the clouds, and it will be the sign of the covenant between me and the earth" (Genesis 9:13).

# Sweet Treat!

**Mealtime Prayer:** Pray this Bible verse: "How sweet are your words to my taste, sweeter than honey to my mouth!" (Psalm 119:103).

**Appetizer:** Did you know that jelly beans, gumdrops, and jawbreakers were invented in the late 1800s during the penny-candy craze? Did you know that there are 40 official Jelly Belly flavors made year round? New flavors are constantly trying to break in. Some of those are kiwi, caramel corn, and French vanilla.[27] What flavor would you invent if you could?

**Dessert Devotion:** Place a bowl of jelly beans (or other small candy) in the center of the table for dessert. Have each person eat one piece. What does it taste like? How does it make your mouth feel? How do kind words sweeten our hearts like candy sweetens our mouths? Read Proverbs 12:25. What does a kind word do?

Now it's time to practice this! Each person takes a turn saying something nice about the family member to his or her left. After one round, switch and go the opposite direction. For each compliment, take two jelly beans.

**Table Talk:**
- How do kind words make you feel?
- What was your favorite compliment? Why?
- How many compliments will you try to give a day?

**Vitamins and Minerals:** "Encourage one another and build each other up, just as in fact you are doing" (1 Thessalonians 5:11).

[27] Jelly Belly home page: http://www.jellybelly.com

**ENCOURAGEMENT/KINDNESS**

# Whatcha Watchin'?

**Mealtime Prayer:** "Lord, strengthen me so that my eyes watch what is good, my heart loves what is good, and my actions display what is good. Amen."

**Appetizer:** Did you know that in 1954 C. A. Swanson & Sons came up with a frozen meal that could easily be heated and eaten in front of the television? It was a complete turkey dinner with an apple-cranberry cobbler.[28] What is your favorite TV dinner?

**TV Dinner:** Fix TV dinners and slide in a favorite movie. A good choice is an *Adventures in Odyssey* episode or a full-length family film such as *Heidi* or the *Jesus* movie. Pay close attention and discuss the film afterward.
- What was the funniest or best part?
- Who was your favorite character? Why?
- Who showed good character? Who showed bad character? How?
- What's one thing in this movie that would please God?

**Table Talk:**
- What was one good example from the movie?
- People watch you just as you watch the examples of others. What can you do to be a good example?
- Who are you an example to?

**Vitamins and Minerals:** "Don't let anyone look down on you because you are young, but set an example for the believers in speech, in life, in love, in faith and in purity" (1 Timothy 4:12).

[28] Food Web site: http://www.gigaplex.com/food/tvdinner

# Index

# Welcome to the Family!

**We hope you've enjoyed this book.** Heritage Builders was founded in 1995 by three fathers with a passion for the next generation. As a new ministry of Focus on the Family, Heritage Builders strives to equip, train and motivate parents to become intentional about building a strong spiritual heritage.

It's quite a challenge for busy parents to find ways to build a spiritual foundation for their families—especially in a way they enjoy and understand. Through activities and participation, children can learn biblical truth in a way they can understand, enjoy—and *remember:*

Passing along a heritage of Christian faith to your family is a parent's highest calling. Heritage Builders' goal is to encourage and empower you in this great mission with practical resources and inspiring ideas that really work—and help your children develop a lasting love for God.

## *How To Reach Us*

For more information, visit our Heritage Builders Web site! Log on to **www.heritagebuilders.com** to discover new resources, sample activities, and ideas to help you pass on a spiritual heritage.

To request any of these resources, simply call Focus on the Family at
1-800-A-FAMILY (1-800-232-6459) or in Canada, call 1-800-661-9800.
Or send your request to Focus on the Family, Colorado Springs, CO 80995. In Canada,
write Focus on the Family, P.O. Box 9800, Stn. Terminal, Vancouver, B.C. V6B 4G3

To learn more about Focus on the Family or to find out if there is         Heritage

# Try These Heritage Builders Resources!

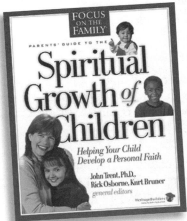

## Parents' Guide to the Spiritual Growth of Children

Building a foundation of faith in your children can be easy–and fun!–with help from the ***Parents' Guide to the Spiritual Growth of Children***. Through simple and practical advice, this comprehensive guide shows you how to build a spiritual training plan for your family and it explains what to teach your children at different ages.

## Family Traditions

Strengthening a family's identity through healthy traditions is key to a godly heritage. In ***Family Traditions,*** find out how to develop a blueprint to bless your children and ensure you are instilling all the qualities you value before they reach adulthood. Paperback.

## My Time With God

Send your child on an amazing adventure—a self-guided tour through God's Word! ***My Time With God*** shows your 8- to 12-year-old how to get to know God regularly in exciting ways. Through 150 days' worth of fun facts and mind-boggling trivia, prayer starters, and interesting questions, your child will discover how awesome God really is!

Heritage Builders

*Helping You Build a Family of Faith*

## The Singing Bible

Children ages 2 to 7 will love *The Singing Bible,* which sets the Bible to music with over 50 fun, sing-along songs! Lead your child through Scripture by using *The Singing Bible* to introduce Jonah and the Whale, the Ten Commandments and more. This is a fun, fast-paced journey kids will remember!

## Joy Ride!

Use your drive time to teach your kids how faith can be part of everyday life with *Joy Ride!* A wonderful resource for parents, this book features activities, puzzles, games and discussion starters to help get your kids thinking about—and living out—what they believe.

• • •

Visit our Heritage Builders Web site!
Log on to **www.heritagebuilders.com** to discover new resources,
sample activities, and ideas to help you pass on a spiritual heritage.
To request any of these resources, simply call Focus on the Family at
1-800-A-FAMILY (1-800-232-6459) or in Canada, call 1-800-661-9800.
Or send your request to Focus on the Family, Colorado Springs, CO 80995. In
Canada, write Focus on the Family,
P.O. Box 9800, Stn. Terminal, Vancouver, B.C. V6B 4G3.

Heritage
Builders
*Helping You Build a Family of Faith*

Every family has a heritage—a spiritual, emotional, and social legacy passed from one generation to the next. There are four main areas we at Heritage Builders recommend parents consider as they plan to pass their faith to their children:

## Family Fragrance

Every family's home has a fragrance. Heritage Builders encourages parents to create a home environment that fosters a sweet, Christ-centered AROMA of love through Affection, Respect, Order, Merriment, and Affirmation.

## Family Traditions

Whether you pass down stories, beliefs and/or customs, traditions can help you establish a special identity for your family. Heritage Builders encourages parents to set special "milestones" for their children to help guide them and move them through their spiritual development.

## Family Compass

Parents have the unique task of setting standards for normal, healthy living through their attitudes, actions and beliefs. Heritage Builders encourages parents to give their children the moral navigation tools they need to succeed on the roads of life.

## Family Moments

Creating special, teachable moments with their children is one of a parent's most precious and sometimes, most difficult responsibilities. Heritage Builders encourages parents to capture little moments throughout the day to teach and impress values, beliefs, and biblical principles onto their children.

Heritage
Builders
*Helping You Build a Family of Faith*

We look forward to standing alongside you as you seek to impart the Lord's care and wisdom onto the next generation—onto your children.

LIGHTwave

building Christian faith in families

**Lightwave Publishing** is one of North America's leading developers of quality resources that encourage, assist, and equip parents to build Christian faith in their families. Its products help parents answer their children's questions about the Christian faith; teach them how to make church, Sunday school, and Bible reading more meaningful for their children; provide them with pointers on teaching their children to pray; and much, much more.

Lightwave, together with its various publishing and ministry partners, such as Focus on the Family, has been successfully producing innovative books, music, and games for the past 15 years. Some of its more recent products include the Parents' *Guide to the Spiritual Growth of Children, Joy Ride!,* and *My Time With God.*

Lightwave also has a fun kids' web site and an Internet-based newsletter called *Tips and Tools for Spiritual Parenting.* For more information and a complete list of Lightwave products, please visit: www.lightwavepublishing.com.